The Look-It-Up Book of
FIRST LADIES

by S. A. Kramer

Random House New York

To the first ladies of my family—Mom, Marion, and Emily.
—S. A. Kramer

The author and editors would like to thank
Craig Schermer of the National First Ladies' Library and
former First Lady Rosalynn Carter for their assistance in the preparation of this book.

Cover photographs:
© Bettmann/CORBIS (J. Kennedy, D. Madison, White House photos, front and back cover); Photograph courtesy F. D. R. Library (E. Roosevelt); © Andrea Renault/Globe Photos, Inc. 2000 (H. Clinton, L. Bush).

Interior photographs: AP/WIDE WORLD PHOTOS, pp. 122, 123, 126, 128; © Bettmann/CORBIS, pp. 9, 10, 12, 13, 14, 15, 18, 19, 20, 21, 22, 23, 26, 27, 28 (bottom), 29, 30, 31, 33 (left and right), 34, 36, 37 (bottom), 39, 41 (right), 43, 44 (right), 45 (bottom), 48, 51 (bottom), 53, 54, 56, 57, 58, 60 (left and right), 62, 63, 64, 65, 66, 67, 69, 72, 73, 77, 83, 85, 89, 91, 93, 103, 110, 120; CORBIS, p. 41 (left), 45 (top), 46, 47, 50, 51 (top), 59, 61, 78, 79, 88; Rick Diamond, p. 4; Dave Edwards/East Hampton Library, p. 35; © FPG International LLC, pp. 17, 25, 80, 106; George Bush Presidential Library, p. 118; © David Muench/CORBIS, p. 16; © Photoworld/FPG International LLC, pp. 40, 52, 86; Pierce Brigade, Concord New Hampshire, p. 44 (left); © Andrea Renault/Globe Photos, Inc. 2000, p. 121, 125; © Reuters NewMedia Inc./CORBIS, p. 117; © Underwood & Underwood/CORBIS, p. 68; © UPI/CORBIS-BETTMANN, pp. 32, 37 (top), 38, 42, 55, 70, 75, 76, 81, 84, 94, 95, 96, 97, 99, 100, 101, 102, 105, 107, 109, 112, 114, 115, 119; © Baldwin H. Ward & Kathryn C. Ward/CORBIS, pp. 24, 28 (top).

Text copyright © 2001 by S. A. Kramer.
Foreword copyright © 2001 by Rosalynn Carter.
All rights reserved under International and Pan-American Copyright Conventions. Published in the United States by Random House, Inc., New York, and simultaneously in Canada by Random House of Canada Limited, Toronto.

www.randomhouse.com/kids

Library of Congress Cataloging-in-Publication Data
Kramer, Sydelle.   The look-it-up book of first ladies / by S.A. Kramer.
    p.   cm.
SUMMARY: Provides profiles of the women who influenced the history of the United States as wives of its presidents.
ISBN 0-679-89347-4 (trade) — ISBN 0-679-99347-9 (lib. bdg.)
1. Presidents' spouses—United States—Biography—Juvenile literature. [1. First ladies. 2. Women—Biography.]
I. Title.   E176.2 .K73   2001   973'.099—dc21   [B]   00-035306
Printed in the United States of America   January 2001   10 9 8 7 6 5 4 3 2 1
RANDOM HOUSE and colophon are registered trademarks of Random House, Inc.

Contents

Foreword	5
Introduction	7
Martha Dandridge Custis Washington	9
Abigail Smith Adams	12
Martha Wayles Skelton Jefferson	15
Dolley Payne Todd Madison	17
Elizabeth Kortright Monroe	20
Louisa Catherine Johnson Adams	22
Rachel Donelson Robards Jackson	25
Hannah Hoes Van Buren	28
Anna Tuthill Symmes Harrison	30
Letitia Christian Tyler	32
Julia Gardiner Tyler	34
Sarah Childress Polk	36
Margaret Mackall Smith Taylor	38
Abigail Powers Fillmore	40
Jane Means Appleton Pierce	42
Harriet Lane Johnston	45
Mary Todd Lincoln	47
Eliza McCardle Johnson	50
Julia Dent Grant	52
Lucy Ware Webb Hayes	55
Lucretia Rudolph Garfield	57
Ellen Lewis Herndon Arthur	59
Frances Folsom Cleveland	61
Caroline Lavinia Scott Harrison	64
Ida Saxton McKinley	67
Edith Kermit Carow Roosevelt	69
Helen Herron Taft	72
Ellen Louise Axson Wilson	75
Edith Bolling Galt Wilson	78
Florence Kling Harding	80
Grace Anna Goodhue Coolidge	83
Lou Henry Hoover	86
Anna Eleanor Roosevelt Roosevelt	89
Elizabeth Virginia Wallace Truman	93
Mamie Geneva Doud Eisenhower	96
Jacqueline Lee Bouvier Kennedy Onassis	99
Claudia Taylor Johnson	103
Thelma Catherine Patricia Ryan Nixon	106
Elizabeth Bloomer Ford	109
Eleanor Rosalynn Smith Carter	112
Anne Frances (Nancy) Robbins Davis Reagan	115
Barbara Pierce Bush	118
Hillary Diane Rodham Clinton	121
Laura Welch Bush	125

Former First Lady Rosalynn Carter

FOREWORD

Being First Lady of the United States was a great honor for me. It was also a huge responsibility. Not many women have such access to the most influential people in government and the media. Even fewer have the opportunity to encourage and stimulate change in our nation. After all, when a First Lady speaks out, people listen.

It is not an easy job. The spotlight always shines on her. She must take care of her family as well as some special needs of the country. As you will read in this book, when First Ladies have heard a call from those who need their help, they have risen to the challenge. I hope these heroic women inspire you to try to rise to your challenge, too.

Every First Lady has had a vision all her own. But we have also had something in common. Each of us has honored her responsibility to her country and to her President. Perhaps someday one of you will have that opportunity, too.

Rosalynn Carter
The Carter Center
Atlanta, Georgia
2000

INTRODUCTION

She's not elected. She's not appointed. She doesn't even get paid for her work. Yet this woman holds one of America's most powerful jobs. She's the wife of the President of the United States, and everyone calls her the First Lady.

She wasn't always known by that term. It was first used in 1849, during Dolley Madison's funeral (at the time, Dolley was the most popular and influential of presidential wives). The term was heard again in the 1860s and '70s, and caught on for good in the early twentieth century. Now the whole world knows who the First Lady is.

Regardless of what she was called, the woman at the President's side has always been in the public spotlight. People notice her style and try to figure out what she's really like. Whatever she says and does affects her husband's popularity. Even the way she wears her hair can gain or cost him votes.

Since Martha Washington's time, First Ladies have defined their role in different ways. Some have devoted themselves to the capital's social life, hosting elegant White House events. Others have been chief advisers to their husbands, helping to shape policy. There have been First Ladies who've courted attention, enjoying the public eye, and others who've avoided it, guarding their privacy.

Some First Ladies have been smarter and better educated than their husbands. Some have barely been able to read. There have been highly ambitious First Ladies who've egged their husbands on to power, and others who've wanted nothing to do with politics. Some have had more money and status than any President. And some have been born into terrible poverty.

Before Eleanor Roosevelt, most First Ladies kept their political opinions private (Abigail Adams was an exception). They were supposed to be model wives and mothers who dressed well and entertained in style. No one expected them to be well schooled or to have careers. Besides, they couldn't. In the eighteenth and nineteenth centuries, even the wealthiest women had few opportunities outside the home. A First Lady might campaign with her husband, but she couldn't cast a ballot in his election! That's because women weren't allowed to vote nationally until 1920.

It was Eleanor who truly brought First Ladies out from behind the scenes. She wasn't afraid to take a public stand on issues, nor to be openly active in politics. Today, no one is surprised if the First Lady states opinions, or at times helps to govern in some way. She can have her own career and even run for President herself.

This book is a history of our Presidents' wives. Some died before their families moved into the White House, but they're here because they contributed to their husbands' careers. Also included are portraits of "substitute" First Ladies—women who helped run the White House if the President was a widower or a bachelor.

Every woman in this book has cut a path through American history. It's safe to say things wouldn't have been quite the same without them. Here are their stories.

MARTHA DANDRIDGE CUSTIS WASHINGTON

wife of the first President, George Washington

Born 1731, died 1802
First Lady 1789–1797

When Martha Washington became the first First Lady of the United States, no one had any idea what the role would require. Martha certainly didn't. She was sure of only one thing—that the First Lady should never act like a Queen. The American people had just fought the Revolutionary War to establish their independence from a monarch. They didn't need the Washingtons behaving like royalty.

Martha worried about her new role. She knew it was up to her to define it. But she was fifty-eight and already a grandmother. Wouldn't a younger woman, she thought, be better at figuring it out? Besides, she had never expected such a responsibility to be hers.

Martha was raised to be a rich planter's wife, not a woman close to political power. Born in Virginia, she was the daughter of a wealthy tobacco grower. Back then, women usually didn't get much education, and Martha was no exception. She never learned to write or spell well, and was so unsure of her grammar that she had someone draft her letters for her. What she did best was ride. She much preferred her horse to a book.

A well-mannered young woman, Martha was nonetheless high-spirited. Once, just for fun, she rode her horse up and down the staircase of her uncle's house. At a ball, she slapped the face of a man she felt was bothering her.

As was the custom of the time, Martha married young. She was only seventeen when she wed Daniel Parke Custis, a wealthy farmer. They had four children, two of whom died. Only eight years into their marriage, Custis died, too. Martha was a widow at the age of twenty-five. She was also one of the richest women in Virginia, with 17,000 acres of fine farmland and several hundred slaves.

A little over a year later, Martha met the soldier and farmer George Washington at dinner at a friend's house. They got along instantly. Just a few days later, they decided to marry. Each of them got something they needed from the match. George benefited from Martha's greater wealth and social position. Martha found a father for her children.

Yet their 1759 marriage was not simply one of convenience—indeed, they loved each other. For the next forty years, George wore a miniature portrait of Martha on a gold chain around his neck. He affectionately called her "Patsy." While they had no children of their own, he adopted hers.

General and Mrs. Washington give a reception in 1789.

Their happy life together at his plantation, Mount Vernon, was interrupted by the Revolution. George became commander in chief of the American forces. But the couple didn't let war separate them. Martha traveled to army camps and spent the winters with George. Short and white-haired, she was so unpretentious she once arrived in camp and was mistaken for a servant. Far from demanding any kind of special treatment, she spent much of her time mending soldiers' clothes and bringing hot soup to the sick and injured. After the war, she became a defender of veterans' rights, raising money to help poor soldiers.

Word spread about Martha Washington's warmth and kindness. Here was a woman without airs who spoke so softly people often couldn't hear her. By the time George became President in 1789, she was a popular figure throughout the country. Her natural dignity and graciousness quickly put people at ease.

Martha had worried for nothing about being First Lady. Still, she didn't find the job simple. She and George didn't even have a real home—there was no White House then. They lived in a small three-story brick house in a poor neighborhood of New York City, at that time the capital of the United States. After a year, the capital—and the Washingtons—moved to Philadelphia. Martha ran the new house, cooking and serving some of the meals by herself, and also hosting a steady stream of receptions.

She had no choice. Martha knew that an active social life was one of the obligations of George's high office. As First Lady, she had to entertain diplomats, politicians, government officials, influential men, and their wives.

George himself requested that she give a party every Friday night. Ever the good wife, she did.

But she had her rules. On those Friday nights, she never once rose from her seat. She ordered the servants to bring the guests to her as they entered. Only after greeting her would they be presented to George. No political discussions were allowed, and the party had to end at 9:00 P.M. sharp—the time Martha insisted that George had to go to bed.

Martha never did learn to enjoy being First Lady. Longing for her lost privacy, she often found herself exhausted by the job's demands. Though she had a mind of her own and an interest in international affairs, she never spoke out. As the President's wife, she felt that she should voice no opinion.

"Lady Washington," as Martha was called, soon grew bored with her job. "I am more like a state prisoner," she complained once, "than anything else." When George left office in 1797, she said the two of them returned to Mount Vernon "like children just released from school."

When George died in 1799, Martha missed him terribly. Not a day went by without her visiting his grave. She was lonely, and welcomed all guests. Politicians would often drop by. Knitting away, she felt free at last to tell them her views on important issues.

When Martha got sick in May 1802, she knew she was dying. Before she took to her bed, she burned all of George's letters to her. Then she picked out the dress in which she wanted to be buried. She had longed, she said, "for the time to follow her departed friend." It had finally arrived.

ABIGAIL SMITH ADAMS

wife of the second President, John Adams

Born 1744, died 1818
First Lady 1797–1801

Abigail Adams was Martha Washington's opposite. No Southern lady born to privilege, Abigail was the daughter of a Massachusetts minister who believed in public service. Like Martha, Abigail didn't go to school, and her spelling and written grammar were poor. But she was a reader. Though it was unusual for a woman to be educated at the time, her father and grandfather taught her philosophy, economics, mathematics, and the classics at home. She was raised to have good manners, but she also spoke her mind.

John Adams took a fancy to Abigail when she was just fourteen. He waited three years, then began to court her actively. But he was a farmer's son, and Abigail's parents didn't think he was good enough for their daughter. It took him another three years to convince them to let him marry her.

Abigail and John wed in 1764, when she was twenty. For their day and age, they had an unusual relationship—a partnership of equals. There were few decisions they didn't make together, even political ones. They seemed always to see things eye to eye.

In the early years of their marriage, they farmed in Massachusetts and had four children. As the struggle between England and its American colonies intensified, the two agreed that John would pursue a political career and actively help the Revolution. Like many other wives of the time, Abigail was in charge of their farm, the family finances, and the kids.

So for the next fifteen years, John was often away. Once, they didn't see each other for four years. While they hated being apart, they both believed serving their country was more important than anything.

The Adams farmhouse in Quincy, Massachusetts

Still, Abigail and John were always in each other's thoughts. Their constant letters contained both pledges of love and debate about the issues of the day. When John was out of the country, he looked to Abigail to keep him informed about politics at home. He called her "my best, dearest, worthiest, wisest friend in this World."

John was George Washington's Vice President, and Abigail found her role as the Vice President's wife boring. Yet when John succeeded George, she was frightened about her new position. After all, she and Martha were so different.

Unlike the older woman, fifty-two-year-old Abigail couldn't play the role of the obedient wife. Although back then women didn't often express political opinions, Abigail had strong views and never hesitated to express them. She believed women were the equals of men and dared to say so. "I will never," she said, "consent to have our sex considered . . . inferior." Bright and well spoken, she wasn't going to change just because she'd become First Lady.

Since Abigail was so "saucy," as John put it, his political enemies called her "Her Majesty" and "Mrs. President." That didn't stop John from consulting her about nearly every issue. She edited his speeches, debated policy with him, and gave him advice. Reporters and politicians were amazed at Abigail's tremendous influence.

Though she was caught up in policy matters, Abigail never neglected the social side of her job. While her opinions made her controversial, she was a successful hostess. Cheerful and optimistic, she was a lively conversationalist. Her dynamic personality helped make her parties a hit.

As First Lady, she needed every bit of her energy. She rose at 5:00 A.M. to run the house. Twice a week, she held receptions. She saw the family through the move from Philadelphia to Washington when that small, muddy town became the new American capital.

In November 1800, Abigail settled the Adamses into a building called the President's House, later to be called the White House. It was still under construction when they arrived—there wasn't even a staircase between the floors. The six rooms that were finished were so cold and damp that Abigail kept thirteen fireplaces burning. It was this miserable new place that Abigail skillfully made the social center of Washington.

When John lost the next election, he and Abigail retired to their Massachusetts farm. Far from the center of power, Abigail was bored. But she took great pleasure in the political success of one of her sons, John Quincy. When he was elected President in 1824, Abigail became the first woman to be both the wife and the mother of a President.

She never stopped speaking out. Her opposition to slavery and her belief in women's equality never wavered. As one who always regretted not going to school,

Portrait of John Adams

she felt strongly that women should have the same educational opportunities as men.

When Abigail died of typhoid at the age of seventy-three, her husband mourned her greatly. So did her fellow citizens. She had shown the country that the wife of the President could be more than a hostess. Through her example, she showed women they had the right to speak their minds. Historians rank her as one of the greatest First Ladies ever.

Martha Jefferson Randolph, President and Mrs. Jefferson's daughter

MARTHA WAYLES SKELTON JEFFERSON

wife of the third President, Thomas Jefferson

Born 1748, died 1782

Poor Martha Jefferson. She died eighteen years before her husband, Thomas Jefferson, was elected President. Her death was a family tragedy—but it may have been fortunate for her country. All those years ago, it was rumored that had she lived, she would never have let Thomas run.

Martha was a wealthy Virginian, a tall woman with reddish-brown hair. An avid reader, she was also a talented musician. When she was eighteen, she married Bathurst Skelton. Two years later, he was dead, and she found herself a wealthy widow.

Many men wanted to marry her in the next three years, but Martha fell in love with Thomas Jefferson. He adored music as much as she did, and particularly admired the way she played the harpsichord. They married in 1772, when she was twenty-three.

It was a time of great political strife, and Thomas was deeply involved in the revolutionary movement. He was often away. Although he begged her to visit him, frail Martha would never go. There were those who suspected she didn't approve of his stand. Others felt she just didn't want him involved in politics. They said that given her poor health, she needed him at home.

Martha herself never discussed politics. Of that, Thomas heartily approved. They both agreed that wives should be devoted to their husbands. That was easy for Martha, since she and Thomas loved each other very much.

In ten years, they had six children. Only two survived. With each birth, Martha grew weaker, until, at age thirty-three, she seemed to wear out. After their last daughter was born, Martha couldn't get out of bed. For four months, she lay ill, slowly fading away.

Thomas spent almost all his time by her bedside. When she died, his grief was so great he didn't leave his room for three weeks. Most of the time he paced back and forth, barely sleeping. He called Martha "the cherished companion of my life."

Later, Thomas destroyed all her letters. He never spoke about her outside the family. Although he lived another forty-four years and had a long relationship with Sally Hemings, his slave (and Martha's half-sister), he never took a second wife. Some people said that was because Martha had asked him never to remarry. Perhaps, though, it was because he felt no one could replace her.

Monticello, the Jeffersons' Virginia estate

DOLLEY PAYNE TODD MADISON

wife of the fourth President, James Madison

Born 1768, died 1849
First Lady 1809–1817

Dolley Madison was the ultimate hostess. No other First Lady has ever been as good at throwing parties. Through her entertaining, she deliberately brought people of different classes and political beliefs together. Her fellow citizens loved her for it. Dolley made them feel good about themselves.

Yet she'd been raised to avoid loud, showy occasions. Born in North Carolina, she was the child of strict Quakers. She was taught to dress simply and sacrifice all comforts. When her grandmother gave her a beautiful gold pin, she knew her parents would disapprove if she put it on. Her solution: wear it where they couldn't see it—*under* her dress!

Dolley's father was a shopkeeper who raised his daughter to be a good wife and mother, nothing more. So like the other women of her day, she didn't get much education. Dolley learned only how to read, write, and do simple sums. When her father's business failed, she became the cook in her mother's boardinghouse.

Then in 1790, she married John Todd, a wealthy lawyer and fellow Quaker. Three years later, a yellow fever epidemic nearly wiped her family out. John and one of their two children died. At the age of twenty-five, she found herself a widow with one son.

Dolley loved people too much to be alone for long. Many men came calling on the widow loaded with warmth and charm. One in particular pursued Dolley intently: Congressman James Madison. He was shorter than her, and seventeen years older. He also wasn't a Quaker.

She hesitated for a bit, then decided. She loved the man she called "Jemmy." (He called her "my beloved.") Less than a year after John's death, Dolley married her "darling little husband." She was ready for the new world of Washington.

At first, the sophisticated capital didn't seem to change Dolley much. But as she grew used to privilege and wealth, she abandoned her modest style, wearing instead bright colors and expensive fabrics. She enjoyed going to parties. Her natural gaiety and love of beauty took over.

Dolley bloomed in Washington. She became more social and helped James's political career. He was often shy and irritable with strangers, while, as Dolley said about herself, "Mrs. Madison loves everybody." At receptions, she charmed even her husband's enemies. When she entertained, Dolley easily mixed politics and friendly conversation, never forgetting a face or name. She often carried a book—or even her parrot—as a means of starting a conversation. People left her parties liking her and admiring James.

By 1801, James was Secretary of State. Dolley had come up in the world, too. The widowed President Jefferson had asked her to act as his hostess. With her dark hair, rosy cheeks, and violet eyes, Dolly was called "the Queen of Washington City." Her parties were the place to be.

James succeeded Jefferson in 1809. By this time, Dolley was so well respected his opponent commented, "I was beaten by Mr. and Mrs. Madison. I might have had a better chance had I faced Mr. Madison alone." First Lady at forty, Dolley was the first wife to attend her husband's swearing-in.

In no time, she made the President's House the center of Washington social life. She redecorated and set trends in fashion and food. Dressed in luxurious gowns and beautiful jewelry, her head adorned by feathered silk turbans, she served her guests French meals and expensive wines.

She also broke social rules. Women weren't supposed to use snuff (tobacco ground into a powder and then inhaled), but Dolley did. Wearing makeup was also discouraged, but Dolley applied rouge. She played cards (and lost) and loved to dance. Her Quaker past seemed a lifetime ago.

Being the world's most famous hostess made Dolley a powerful First Lady. While she didn't try to influence policy, she used her parties to gather political information for her husband, and to

Dolley Madison saved the Declaration of Independence from the burning White House during the War of 1812.

flatter and soothe his enemies. Her weekly Wednesday reception was so popular it was nicknamed "Mrs. Madison's Crush." There powerful politicians and diplomats mixed with office workers and artists. Men and women chatted together instead of separating into different rooms. Dolley greeted all her guests personally, making each one feel important.

She became the most popular person in America. The press followed her every move. Energetic and well spoken, she was the first presidential wife to give an official interview to a reporter.

And all the while, she and James enjoyed a happy marriage. Whenever they were apart, they wrote each other long, loving letters. But despite their affection, they had no children.

By James's second term, Dolley had become a role model for American women. Then, on August 24, 1814, she became more—a true hero. Britain and America were fighting the War of 1812. It was a time of bloody battles. Determined to destroy Washington, the British advanced on the city. Most residents fled. Not Dolley.

James was away visiting American troops. Dolley expected him back shortly and wouldn't leave without him. Grabbing a pair of binoculars, she raced to the roof of the President's House to watch for his return.

But the British arrived first. Dolley didn't panic. She went from room to room in the President's House to save its most historically precious items. She packed the original copies of the Constitution and Declaration of Independence in her trunk. She gave the portrait of George Washington by the famous artist Gilbert Stuart to friends escaping to New York.

Portrait of James Madison

Coolheaded as ever, Dolley disguised herself to get away. Dressed as a farmer's wife, she fled Washington in a carriage. As she left, the city was burning. Soon the President's House itself went up in flames.

The British didn't stay long, and Dolley quickly returned. When word spread that she'd saved part of America's heritage from destruction, she said, "Anyone would have done what I did."

When the war was finally over, Dolley celebrated by throwing one of her best parties ever. Even after she left Washington, she continued to entertain. People from all over the world came to Montpelier, James's Virginia estate, just to attend one of Dolley's events.

She never lost her touch, or her influence. After her husband's death, she returned to Washington, where the nation's most powerful politicians came to call. Soon she was known as "Queen Dolley."

Still, her old age was difficult. Her son was an alcoholic who frittered away her fortune. When Congress finally came to her rescue by buying important papers James had written, she did what came naturally—threw a party!

ELIZABETH KORTRIGHT MONROE

wife of the fifth President, James Monroe

Born 1768, died 1830
First Lady 1817–1825

Long before she became First Lady, Elizabeth Monroe was a heroine like Dolley Madison. She saved a woman's life in Paris, where she lived when James Monroe was America's ambassador to France. *"La belle Américaine,"* as she was known there, was admired for her dark-haired beauty and charm.

It was 1795, a time when the French Revolution had given way to the years known as the Reign of Terror. Aristocrats were arrested, then guillotined, often just because of their class. Until Elizabeth got involved, it seemed that that would be the fate of the wife of the Marquis de Lafayette (a champion of the American Revolution).

Elizabeth and James had a plan. They felt the French wouldn't dare execute Madame Lafayette if the American ambassador's wife paid her a visit. So a daring Elizabeth went to see her in prison.

A crowd stood nearby while Elizabeth embraced Madame Lafayette. Everyone heard Elizabeth say loudly that she'd be back to see her friend the next day. French officials, who'd planned on killing the woman that very afternoon, released her instead. Elizabeth's visit had saved the woman's life!

But by the time Elizabeth became First Lady over twenty years later, most Americans had forgotten her heroic act. What they remembered was her wealthy New York background and her father's support for the British during the Revolution. To the average person, her perfect French and preference for Parisian clothes made her seem snobbish. Elegant Elizabeth, they thought, was haughty and cold.

Her own behavior didn't help. She decorated the rebuilt President's House (its outside walls now painted all white) more like a European palace than an American home. Her exquisite dresses and expensive taste led people to feel she wanted to be Queen.

Elizabeth knew that Washington society was comparing her to Dolley Madison. But she was a private person who hated to entertain and stubbornly ignored Dolley's example. She skipped her husband's inaugural ball and stayed away from most parties. At the few she attended, she rarely spoke. When her daughter Maria wed in the White House (as the building was becoming known), she left the wedding plans to Maria's older sister, Eliza Monroe Hays. She, truly a snob, ignored all political obligations and kept the wedding private. Not a single politician or official was invited. People of influence were enraged at the snub.

Elizabeth made them even more furious by not returning visits. Unlike Dolley, she hated the Washington custom of paying endless calls. Her reluctance to do so benefited future First Ladies, however, who after Elizabeth were freed from this duty. Unfortunately for Elizabeth, though, it merely increased her unpopularity.

Yet no amount of criticism made Elizabeth question her decisions. During James's second term in office, she left the city for months at a time to visit their two daughters. That left no hostess in the White House. Since the social rules of the day prevented women from attending parties in such circumstances, only men could go to White House events. Washington wives were furious.

Elizabeth often claimed illness to explain her behavior. Few people,

Portrait of James Monroe

though, believed she was seriously sick. Forty-nine years old when James took office, Elizabeth simply looked too young and healthy.

But Elizabeth had a secret. She probably had epilepsy, a disease that affects the brain and causes seizures. Once she was stricken so suddenly that she fell into a fireplace and was burned. Most people were frightened of epilepsy back then, so the Monroes didn't reveal what was wrong.

When James left office, he and Elizabeth retired to their Virginia home, Oak Hill. There she got sicker and sicker and died at age sixty-three. She'd been a public person most of her life, but her country hardly knew her. In fact, she was so private that only one letter from her has survived. Elizabeth would have wanted it that way.

LOUISA CATHERINE JOHNSON ADAMS

wife of the sixth President, John Quincy Adams

Born 1775, died 1852
First Lady 1825–1829

Luckily, Louisa Adams had a very happy childhood. She needed those memories of love and warmth to get her through most of her marriage. John Quincy was a distant man absorbed in his career. Although she was vital to his success, he rarely showed his appreciation.

The only First Lady to be an American citizen born outside the United States (in London, England), Louisa was the daughter of wealthy parents. They doted on her, raising her in Europe and sending her to good schools in England and France. Intellectually inclined, she was an eager reader and an excellent musician. She also learned exquisite manners (developing social skills Elizabeth Monroe might have envied).

Louisa met John Quincy Adams when he was a diplomat in London. She liked the stern young man but hated his sloppy clothes. When they were courting, they argued about how he dressed. It was the first disagreement of many to come.

They married in 1797, the year John Quincy's father became President. The couple stayed abroad, as ambitious John Quincy worked there for his father. Four years later, when Louisa was twenty-six, they moved to America. It was the first time she'd set foot in her own country.

Right away, there was trouble. John Quincy's mother, Abigail Adams, didn't like her. Louisa wasn't American enough—to Abigail, she seemed like a foreigner. So John Quincy often visited his family on his own, leaving Louisa alone for months.

He proved to be an insensitive, self-absorbed husband. Within the marriage, he was more a tyrant than a partner. He expected Louisa to do what he said, despite what she thought. Not once did he consult her, even about matters affecting her. They ended up arguing about everything, from how to raise their three sons to whether she could wear rouge to parties.

Yet all the while, John Quincy's career prospered. From 1797 to 1801, he was a diplomat in Prussia (the most powerful state in eighteenth-century Germany), and Louisa was pleased to be in the Europe she loved. During John Quincy's

Woodcut of a ball given by Louisa Adams at the White House.
John Quincy Adams is shown at the far right, and Andrew Jackson is at the center.

term in the U.S. Senate (1802–1808), she enjoyed Washington. But everything changed when he became ambassador to Russia. Without asking her opinion, he sent their two oldest boys away to his parents in Massachusetts. Only the youngest came with them to Russia.

Louisa was crushed. She missed the children terribly. The freezing Russian winters made her physically sick. Worse, the baby girl she gave birth to there died from the cold.

Six years passed before the family was reunited. Louisa's health became worse and worse. Since her marriage, she'd been pregnant twelve times but had seven miscarriages. The severe Russian climate weakened her further.

Despite John Quincy's coldness, Louisa knew he needed her. When James Monroe appointed him Secretary of State, she overcame her natural shyness and made herself Washington's best hostess. Like Dolley Madison before her, she used her parties to help her husband politically. Her events were so popular that other hostesses copied them.

John Quincy may have been the politician of the family, but Louisa was the one most people liked. That's why he asked her to make up to twenty-five visits a day requesting influential people to support his presidential run. She hated these visits, commenting, "I really sometimes think they will make me crazy." But she made them all the same.

When John Quincy took office, Louisa was fifty and in poor health. But he nonetheless demanded that she be an active hostess. Honoring her obligations, she never missed a social engagement. To the delight of her guests, she'd often play the harp and piano to entertain them.

But away from the parties, Louisa often found herself alone. She and John Quincy had long separations in which they exchanged such formal letters that they both signed their full names. When they were together, they saw each other only for meals, reading their newspapers instead of speaking. Now that he was President, John Quincy ignored her.

Louisa became depressed. She called herself "a prisoner in my own house." It didn't help that John Quincy grew so unpopular that most of her entertaining came to a halt. There she was in the White House, lonely and bored. To pass the time, she stuffed herself with chocolate and wrote poetry and plays. She even turned out an autobiography she entitled *The Diary of a Nobody.*

In the last year of John Quincy's term, their oldest son died. It was rumored that he'd killed himself. The couple's grief brought them together, and their marriage finally improved, even more so after they left the White House.

John Quincy was elected to Congress. Helping out in his office, Louisa got involved in his causes. Both of them became abolitionists (people who wanted to end slavery) and also fought for the rights of women. It had taken many years, but they had a partnership at last.

Engraving of John Quincy Adams

RACHEL DONELSON ROBARDS JACKSON

wife of the seventh President, Andrew Jackson

Born 1767, died 1828

Rachel and Andrew Jackson's marriage couldn't have been more different from Louisa and John Quincy Adams's. Theirs was one of the greatest presidential romances. Yet scandal plagued them from the time they met, and rumors, false accusations, and snobbery brought their love story to a tragic end.

Rachel Jackson's life started out simply enough. Born in Virginia, she was one of eleven children of a respected family. Raised on what was then the frontier, she grew up with no school nearby. While she could read and write, she never got much education. Her teenage years, in Tennessee, were instead devoted to riding and dancing. By the age of seventeen, the creamy-skinned young woman had high spirits, good looks, and the ability to entertain friends with spellbinding tales.

Then she made a huge mistake. Still a teenager, she married a Kentuckian named Lewis Robards in 1785. He turned out to be vicious and violent, a jealous husband who criticized her every move. Rachel was terrified of him and relieved when he threw her out. He thought better of it later, but she'd already fled. After a while, Robards announced he would divorce her.

Rachel was delighted. By this time, she'd fallen in love with Andrew Jackson. He'd been rooming at her mother's boardinghouse, the first place she stayed after leaving Robards. He'd helped her get down the Mississippi River, protecting her from Indian attack. After pledging his love to the beautiful woman, Andrew waited faithfully for her divorce to come through. In 1791, the two got word that it finally had. When they quickly married, it seemed that only happiness could follow.

But two years later, Rachel and Andrew discovered they'd made a mistake. Robards had *not* divorced her, and their marriage was illegal. People began to gossip about Rachel, as though she had deliberately done something wrong. When the divorce was finally issued, she and Andrew remarried in a quiet second ceremony. But the attacks on Rachel's reputation continued.

For the next thirty-four years, a protective Andrew often had to defend his wife's good name. There were many fights, even a duel in which he killed a man who'd insulted her. For her part, Rachel was totally devoted to him.

It was a good thing, since marriage to Andrew wasn't always easy. He was a military man in a time of frequent battles, and also a politician dedicated to his career. That meant the couple was often separated, with Rachel left to run their Tennessee plantation, the Hermitage. It was a lonely life—they had no children to keep her company. Eventually, they adopted one of her nephews. Rachel turned more and more to religion, never leaving home without her Bible.

When Andrew became a powerful senator, the attacks on Rachel grew fiercer. His political enemies gossiped about the divorce and criticized her lack of education. The wife of a prominent man, they said, should be sophisticated and well traveled, not a simple woman raised on the frontier.

Washington society looked down on her. Ignoring her warmth and generosity, it mocked her for smoking a pipe. People laughed at her lined, rough skin, and her riding a horse instead of sitting in a carriage. As she got older, she put on weight. One cruel partygoer called her "a short, fat dumpling. . . ." Rachel felt so

Engraving of Andrew Jackson

badly about the insults that when she was in Washington, she wouldn't leave the house.

She hated politics. A private person, she couldn't understand why people would spread lies. She wanted Andrew to quit public life so they could be together at home. Once she wrote him, "You have served your country long enough." But he wanted to be President.

During his campaign, criticism of Rachel mounted. One newspaper said she was "not a suitable person to be placed at the head of the female society of the United States." When Andrew was elected, she commented, ". . . for Mr. Jackson's sake I am glad . . . but for myself I am not." She didn't want to live in "that palace," as she called the White House. But she knew she had to. If she stayed in Tennessee, it would look as if she were afraid of her critics. Besides, she would miss Andrew terribly.

So Rachel got herself ready to become First Lady. She bought a new wardrobe, and a white satin gown for the inaugural ball. But before she could get to Washington, tragedy struck. On

Engraving of Rachel Jackson

December 22, 1828, she had a heart attack and died.

Only sixty-one, Rachel was buried in her new gown. Ten thousand people came to her funeral. Andrew himself wrote the inscription on her tomb: "A being so gentle and virtuous, slander might wound but could not dishonor."

He went to Washington a bitter man, believing to the end it was the scandal that had killed her. Every day, he wore a miniature portrait of her around his neck. To honor her publicly, he planted beautiful magnolia trees near the southwest corner of the White House.

Rachel's twenty-two-year-old niece, Emily Donelson, came to Washington to be Andrew's hostess. Lovely though she was, she was no replacement for Rachel. Andrew never stopped thinking of his wife, always believing she died of a broken heart.

HANNAH HOES VAN BUREN

wife of the eighth President, Martin Van Buren

Born 1783, died 1819

Hannah Van Buren died of tuberculosis eighteen years before her husband, Martin Van Buren, was elected President. So little is known about her, not even her sons knew for sure if her name was Hannah or Anna. Martin didn't help to fill in the missing facts when he failed to mention her even once in his eight-hundred-page autobiography!

What's certain is that the two were born in the same small town in New York and attended school together. When Hannah was twenty-four, she and Martin married. They were both of Dutch heritage and often spoke the language at home. The Van Burens had five sons, one of whom died in infancy. Hannah was not yet thirty-six at the time of her death. An article in the Albany *Argus* called her "an ornament of the Christian faith."

Hannah was a sweet, modest woman of strong religious beliefs. Letters indicate

Portrait of Martin Van Buren

Angelica Van Buren, Martin Van Buren's daughter-in-law,
acted as his White House hostess.

that she was busy, sociable, and happy.

She was known in the community for her concern for the poor. In contrast, Angelica Singleton Van Buren, the daughter-in-law who would eventually step in for her as Martin's White House hostess, was thought by many Americans to be a pretentious spendthrift.

Yet Angelica, a relative of Dolley Madison (who masterminded the romance between Angelica and Abraham Van Buren, Hannah and Martin's oldest son), was much admired for her looks. A twenty-four-year-old from South Carolina, she had big brown eyes, a small waist, and dark brown hair that fell in ringlets down her back. As though she herself were impressed by her own beauty, she acted like the royalty she had met on her European honeymoon, even trying to turn the White House into a palace. At her parties, she sat like a Queen on a raised platform, surrounded by ladies-in-waiting. Always dressed in expensive gowns, she greeted guests with three ostrich feathers in her hair. This kind of behavior was called "Queen Fever."

Hannah's style would have been much simpler. Had she lived, Martin's White House would have been a place of dignity.

ANNA TUTHILL SYMMES HARRISON

wife of the ninth President, William Henry Harrison

Born 1775, died 1864
First Lady 1841

Anna Harrison never wanted her husband to be President. For years, she looked forward to retiring quietly with him to their Ohio farm. When he decided to run, it seemed she knew it would lead to sorrow.

Since Anna's childhood, death had been a constant presence in her life. The well-educated daughter of a New Jersey judge, she lost her mother when she was little. Raised by her grandparents (her father was off fighting in the Revolution), she grew up to be a beautiful young woman. But she'd been touched early by tragedy and viewed life very seriously.

When Anna was nineteen, her father moved to Ohio, where Anna joined him and her stepmother. From there, she went to visit her sister in Kentucky and met William Henry Harrison. They were soon taken with each other,

but her father didn't approve—William was a soldier. That wasn't enough to stop Anna, however. She had a mind of her own, and the next time her father went away on business, she called in a justice of the peace and married her soldier.

Over the years, "Pah," as Anna called William, was in and out of the army, rising to the rank of general and also holding political posts such as governor of Indiana. They moved often, and William spent much of the time away. Anna was frequently on her own with their ten children.

Her life was hectic. She educated her children herself, also tutoring most of her neighbors' kids. A religious woman, she was so involved with her church that every Sunday she'd have the whole congregation over to dinner. She pursued her interests in politics and reading, eagerly poring over every newspaper she could find. A lively conversationalist, she loved company and always seemed to be entertaining. But death continued to shadow her—four of her children died young.

Anna was proud of her husband's military accomplishments, but when he retired from the army, she was delighted to have him for herself. He didn't stay home long, however. The Whigs convinced him to run for President. Ever the loyal wife, sixty-five-year-old Anna helped his campaign by throwing parties for his supporters.

Then tragedy struck again. A fifth child died. Anna grew so depressed she stopped appearing in public. When William won the election, all she could say was, "I wish that my husband's friends had left him where he is, happy and contented in his retirement."

The oldest First Lady ever, Anna fell ill that winter. When William left for Washington in 1841, she stayed home on the advice of doctors. By the time she was well enough to travel, William was sick with pneumonia. Death came to him so quickly he died before she could reach him.

Anna lived another twenty-four years. In her long life, she was in mourning many times. By the time of her own death at eighty-eight, only one of her ten children, a son, was still alive. She most likely wouldn't have been pleased that *his* son Benjamin, her grandchild, became the twenty-third President of the United States.

William Henry Harrison died only one month after his inauguration.

LETITIA CHRISTIAN TYLER

first wife of the tenth President, John Tyler

Born 1790, died 1842
First Lady 1841–1842

John Tyler might never have been President if it hadn't been for his wife Letitia Tyler. The daughter of a rich Virginia planter, she had great wealth and social position. John used them both to his advantage. Married in 1813 after a five-year engagement, Letitia managed their plantation (and slaves) while John pursued his political career. The money she made through her business skills and wise investments increased their wealth and made him a powerful political figure.

That pleased Letitia. She took pride in her John. While she was shrewd and intelligent, she was "perfectly content," one writer said, "to be seen only as a part of the existence of her beloved husband." A shy, quiet woman devoted to her religion, she was not eager to become part of Washington society. Even after John was elected to the U.S. Senate, she remained in Virginia to raise their five children.

Three years before John became President, Letitia had a stroke. It left her unable to talk or walk. Over time she learned to speak again, but she had to use a wheelchair for the rest of her life. Her mind, though, was as sharp as ever, and she spent much of her time reading.

John was William Henry Harrison's Vice President and succeeded him when he died. Fifty-year-old Letitia was unexpectedly First Lady. Because of her disability, she did not act as her husband's hostess. She left that job to her daughter-in-law, Priscilla Cooper Tyler, a very respected Shakespearean actress. Moving into the White House with some of her slaves, Letitia spent her days upstairs, coming down only once, to attend her daughter's wedding.

Priscilla met the demands of being

White House hostess with spirit and success. An intelligent and beautiful woman with brown hair, she charmed the President's guests and enjoyed the expert advice of Dolley Madison. Behind the scenes, though, Letitia continued to help John. From her bed, she planned the social life of the White House and ran the family. At times she even advised her husband politically. One of her daughters remarked, "I have frequently heard our father say that he rarely failed to consult her judgment in the midst of difficulties and troubles. . . ."

But Letitia's illness finally got the best of her. The first First Lady to die in the White House, she passed away on September 10, 1842, holding a damask rose in her hand. She was taken to Virginia to be buried at the plantation where she was born.

John Tyler became President upon the death of William Henry Harrison.

Priscilla Cooper Tyler, the President's daughter-in-law, acted as White House hostess while his wife, Letitia, was ill.

JULIA GARDINER TYLER

second wife of John Tyler

Born 1820, died 1889
First Lady 1844–1845

First Lady for just eight months, Julia Tyler was the opposite of Letitia Tyler. Her glamour and high spirits made her a popular hostess. John Tyler was lucky to win her hand—two congressmen and a Supreme Court justice also proposed to her. High-society Julia was considered quite a catch.

She was born in New York to a family so wealthy they owned their own island. They gave her a good education and the best of everything. The President fell in love with the sophisticated twenty-three-year-old as they played cards at a White House dinner her family attended. Two weeks later, he proposed, but the "Rose of Long Island" turned him down.

For over a year, John pursued Julia, although he was more than thirty years her senior. After her father's sudden death, she agreed to wed, and in 1844, the two eloped. John thus became the first President to marry while in office.

Right away, Julia took charge of the President's social life. She gave parties as though the White House were a palace. Wearing a headdress that looked like a crown, she greeted guests from a large armchair atop a raised platform. Twelve women in matching dresses surrounded "Her Serene Loveliness," as Julia was called. Whenever she went out, she traveled in a fancy coach pulled by six white horses.

Some criticized Julia for being extravagant and pretentious. But her humor, charm, and good looks won her many friends. She thrived on attention and went so far as to hire a press agent to make sure she got favorable publicity.

In her short time in the White House, she wielded a lot of influence. Like Dolley Madison, she used social events to affect policy—a party she threw for two

Gardiner's Island, owned by Julia Gardiner's family

thousand people helped build momentum for the annexation of Texas. Calling herself "Mrs. President Tyler," she began the tradition of playing "Hail to the Chief" at the President's appearances.

When John lost his reelection bid, she was terribly upset. She dressed in black from head to toe the day she left the White House. The couple moved to John's Virginia plantation, where they had seven children. Northerner Julia became so Southern she supported the Confederacy during the Civil War.

One night in 1862, Julia had a terrible dream. In it, her husband was deathly ill. Her dream turned out to be true, and in a few days, he was dead. She lived another twenty-seven years, always faithful to his memory.

SARAH CHILDRESS POLK

wife of the eleventh President, James Polk

Born 1803, died 1891
First Lady 1845–1849

Sarah Polk wanted to be First Lady. The dark-haired daughter of a rich Tennessee planter, she was smart and well read at a time when women had few intellectual opportunities. Since she couldn't be politically ambitious for herself (women couldn't hold office—or even vote—back then), she wanted to marry a man who would go far. Not until James Polk won an election would she become his wife.

His family wasn't especially happy with his choice of bride—tall, thin Sarah was too independent for their liking. In an age when women considered caring for family and home their most important tasks, Sarah wouldn't manage a household and didn't have children. She dared to say, "I will neither keep house, nor make butter. . . ."

From the first days of their marriage, she and James were very close. They shared an interest in politics, and Sarah helped him in all stages of his career. She even managed his campaign for governor of Tennessee behind the scenes. With her eye on the White House, she pushed him to run for higher office.

Back then, women didn't speak freely in public about their views. Sarah was different—she said what she thought. But to avoid offending people and costing James votes, she always prefaced her ideas by saying, "Mr. Polk believes. . . ." Some observers thought James was under her thumb, but Sarah was so elegant and gracious most found her charming.

She came to the White House politically sophisticated but with strict religious beliefs. When she arrived at James's inaugural ball, the orchestra stopped playing because she didn't approve of dancing. She wouldn't go to the theater, or a concert, or a horse race, and didn't allow hard liquor or card-playing in her presence. Yet her religion didn't stop her from dressing in expensive low-cut velvet gowns, or from running the Polk cotton plantations with hundreds of slaves. She even brought slaves with her to the White House.

Forty-one when she became First Lady, Sarah worked hard at the job. As James's closest adviser, she shared his office and worked by his side twelve hours a day. A workaholic couple, they never took vacations.

Sarah attended congressional debates and read through newspapers to cut out articles she thought James should read. He relied on her to research issues and write his speeches. "None but Sarah," he once said, "knew so intimately my private affairs."

Politics fascinated her. At official dinners, she'd sometimes forget to eat because she was so involved in discussing an issue. During White House receptions, she'd debate politics with the men instead of doing what was expected—making

James Polk's tomb

small talk with the women. As her husband did, she believed fiercely in both slavery and Manifest Destiny (the right of America to expand into and absorb new territories, such as Texas and California).

After leaving office, James died suddenly at the age of fifty-four. Sarah lived another forty-two years, but she never remarried. Although visitors were welcome, she hardly ever left the house. Focused on preserving her husband's memory, she made a museum out of their home, placing his marble tomb right on the front lawn. So devoted was she to the dead man that she said, "Life was . . . a blank" once he'd passed away.

Daguerreotype portrait of James Polk. The daguerreotype was an early form of photography invented in France in 1837.

This portrait is believed by many historians to be Margaret Taylor.

MARGARET (PEGGY) MACKALL SMITH TAYLOR

wife of the twelfth President, Zachary Taylor

Born 1788, died 1852
First Lady 1849–1850

Peggy Taylor had a lot in common with Anna Harrison. She endured the hard life of a soldier's wife, dreaming of a peaceful retirement that never came.

Born in Maryland to a prominent farming family, Peggy was a proper Southern lady. But her privileged life ended when she visited her sister in Kentucky and met Zachary Taylor. Her family disapproved of him because he was a soldier, but twenty-one-year-old Peggy married him anyway. She spent the next forty years living on army posts in some of the most remote and dangerous places in America, learning to nurse the wounded and use a gun during Indian raids. Zachary commented, "My wife was as much of a soldier as I was."

It was a hard, lonely existence. The couple had six children, three of whom died young. At times, there wasn't even a house for them to live in, only a tent or small log cabin. Zachary became a general, but Peggy's health suffered. She never considered leaving, though— she felt her place was at her husband's side.

By the time she was sixty, Peggy was anxious to retire. She wanted a quiet life in a cottage away from soldiers, battles, and forts. When Zachary was elected President, she was so unhappy she refused to act as First Lady. Her twenty-two-year-old daughter Betty acted as Zachary's hostess.

Peggy was in no rush to get to Washington. She arrived (with her slaves) just in time for Zachary's inauguration. By now her health was so poor she spent most days upstairs in the White House, leaving only to attend church.

Zachary Taylor fought in the War of 1812 and was an outstanding commander in the Mexican War.

But there was another reason Peggy shut herself away—she wanted to avoid publicity. Although she occasionally attended an official dinner or helped Zachary entertain, she was such a private person she refused to sit for her White House portrait. Most Americans had no idea what she looked like, and she wanted to keep it that way.

Peggy didn't end up living long in Washington. Zachary died of heat stroke after just sixteen months in office. Grief-stricken, she lay in bed, refusing to speak. She never once referred to the White House after she left it. Two years later, she, too, was dead.

ABIGAIL POWERS FILLMORE

wife of the thirteenth President, Millard Fillmore

Born 1798, died 1853
First Lady 1850–1853

Abigail Fillmore's life was a classic American success story. She was born into poverty in New York, yet ended up in the White House. She was the first presidential wife to come from a penniless background.

Abigail's father, a minister, died when she was two. Her mother taught school and took in boarders to support the family. Determined to give Abigail an education, she taught her herself at home.

Abigail followed in her mother's footsteps. By the age of sixteen, she'd become a teacher in love with learning and books. Three years later, the tall, blue-eyed, red-haired young woman developed another passion—for a teenaged pupil of hers, Millard Fillmore. In just a few months they were engaged.

Eight years would pass, though, before they married. Millard went off to law school, and Abigail didn't see him for three long years. They had no money for travel, and instead wrote each other letters constantly.

Abigail missed her fiancé, but at least she had her books. Continuing to teach, she started the first public library in the small town of Sempronius, New York. Even after she and Millard finally wed in 1826, she kept her job and filled their small home with books. When Millard was elected to the state assembly, she finally stopped teaching—but not learning. She taught herself French, played the piano, and eagerly read whatever Millard bought her when he was away. That, plus their two children, filled her days.

As Millard rose to higher office, Abigail found herself with a new interest: politics. The couple was so close that Millard consulted her on the important issues of the day. After all, it had been her teaching that had started him on his career. But by the time Millard became Zachary Taylor's Vice President, Abigail's health was so poor she couldn't accompany him to Washington.

After Zachary's death, Millard became President. Despite her weak condition, Abigail moved into the White House. One of her first concerns upon arriving was the scarcity of books. Choosing the volumes herself, she began the first White House library.

Fifty-two by now, she was hobbled by an old ankle injury that made it painful for her to stand. So she refused all outside invitations. Her eighteen-year-old daughter was often her substitute at events. But when receptions were held at the White House, she found she could attend if she stayed in bed all day. It seemed she didn't mind much—she got the chance to read.

A witty, intelligent woman, Abigail was friendly with many of America's most famous writers. She followed legislative debates and was known for her anti-slavery position. Because she was so well informed, a friend said that Millard "never took any important step without her counsel and advice."

Abigail's life ended shortly after Millard's term in office. She caught a terrible chill at Franklin Pierce's inauguration and died of pneumonia.

Portrait of Abigail Fillmore

Millard Fillmore became President after Zachary Taylor's death.

JANE MEANS APPLETON PIERCE

wife of the fourteenth President, Franklin Pierce

Born 1806, died 1863
First Lady 1853–1857

A sad woman of intensely religious beliefs, Jane Pierce never got over the death of her beloved son Bennie. The accident that killed the boy happened just two months before Franklin Pierce's inauguration, and she blamed the election for it. Politics was an evil profession, she felt, and God was punishing her and her family for Franklin's success.

Jane had inherited her passionate faith from her father. He was a college president and minister who was also a spiritual fanatic. He died while fasting, or refusing to eat, when Jane was just thirteen. Her mother, nearly as devout, made sure Jane received a religious education.

Two different stories are told about how young Jane and Franklin first met. One has it that she was frightened during a thunderstorm and huddled under a tree when he ran out of the library (he was then a law student) and came to her rescue. The other puts Jane in a broken-down stagecoach with Franklin fixing its wheel, barely able to take his eyes off her. After all, with her fine white skin and rich, reddish-brown hair, Jane was quite attractive. However it really happened, the two fell in love, even though they were complete opposites. Shy, sickly Jane was prim and proper, while warm, outgoing Franklin liked to have a good time. Despite their differences, they decided to marry.

It was a long engagement. Over seven years passed before they wed in 1834. By then, ambitious Franklin had been elected to Congress, a career Jane disapproved of. Their marriage was rocky. The two often argued. He ended up spending most of his time in Washington, where he led an active social life, while Jane stayed at home in New

Hampshire, a place she felt was better suited to raising children. She was also so ill with tuberculosis by this time that she was unable to take care of the house.

The couple's years apart were hard for Jane. Franklin began to have a drinking problem. Two of their three sons died very young. At last, Jane convinced her husband to abandon politics and return to New Hampshire. It turned out to be a good move. They spent happy years together there as he settled into a successful law practice. An attentive mother, Jane devoted herself to her remaining son.

When the Mexican War was declared in 1846, Franklin went to fight. He came home a general, a hero, and a strong presidential contender. When the Democrats nominated him, Jane fainted from despair. She prayed for him to be defeated. Franklin only took the nomination because of the benefits it would reap for Bennie later in life.

Soon after he was elected, the family was aboard a train that ran off the tracks. Jane and Franklin were unharmed, but eleven-year-old Bennie was crushed to death. Jane, just forty-six, never recovered from her grief.

She was so depressed that she couldn't act as First Lady. A friend of hers took her

The Pierce residence in Concord, New Hampshire

Jane Pierce never got over the death of her son Bennie.

Portrait of Franklin Pierce

place at White House events. Close to madness, she locked herself in her room and wrote letters to Bennie, pouring out all the repressed love she could never express in person. People began to call her the "Shadow of the White House." One visitor said, "Her woebegone face, with its sunken dark eyes, and skin like yellow ivory, banished all animation in others." No one could have been more patient or loving than her husband.

Nearly two years passed before Jane tried to host parties. Even then, as one reporter wrote, "Her efforts to entertain were forced and gave only pain to those who attended her receptions. Everything seemed to partake of her own serious melancholy and mournful feelings."

Her spirits didn't improve with the passage of time. After Franklin left office, they frequently traveled, but Jane kept a box containing locks of her children's hair by her side at all times. Her last words welcomed death: "Other refuge have I none."

HARRIET LANE JOHNSTON

niece of the fifteenth President, James Buchanan

Born 1830, died 1903
First Lady 1857–1861

An orphan from the age of ten, Harriet Johnston was well cared for by her bachelor guardian, the future President James Buchanan. Uncle James treated her like a daughter, sparing no expense and sending her to the best boarding schools. Not a week would go by without a letter from "Nunc," as Harriet called him. She went to England with him when he was appointed ambassador and hosted his receptions. He often confided in her his longing to be President.

James Buchanan's wish came true in 1857. The only unmarried president in history, he called on violet-eyed Harriet to be his official hostess. She was just twenty-seven when she gave her first White House party, but she had the sophistication and vision of a more experienced woman. The North and South were on the verge of civil war, but Harriet had a way of making sure all social occasions went smoothly—she forbade political talk by her guests.

She had another rule, too—people at her parties were expected to dress well.

Engraving of James Buchanan

45

Painting of James Buchanan and the Prince of Wales visiting Washington's tomb

Harriet herself was a fashion plate. With her silky blond hair decorated with fancy ornaments, she wore white clothing with low necklines and huge full skirts. Soon, the women of Washington were copying her style.

But Harriet wasn't interested in only the social scene. Every morning she and James read the newspapers together. A serious young woman, she believed strongly in rights for American Indians. Highly cultured, she was an art collector and the first First Lady to invite prominent artists to presidential dinners.

Five years after she left the White House, Harriet married Henry Elliott Johnston, a wealthy banker. She continued to buy paintings throughout her life, amassing an impressive collection. When she died, she generously left it to the National Gallery of Art.

MARY TODD LINCOLN

wife of the sixteenth President, Abraham Lincoln

Born 1818, died 1882
First Lady 1861–1865

Mary Lincoln was one of the most controversial of First Ladies, overseeing the White House during the Civil War and managing to offend both sides. It may well be that no presidential wife could have fared better during such ugly times, but Mary's personality and emotional difficulties contributed to her problems. She was also supremely unlucky—tragedy shadowed even her triumphs and eventually wore her down.

Her bad fortune began in childhood. Born to a prosperous Kentucky family, little Mary seemed headed for an easy life. But her mother died when she was nearly seven. Things were never the same. Her father's second wife was an uncaring stepmother. Although Mary still had the best of everything, including an excellent education, it came without love. She was sent away to boarding school and spent little time with her family.

On the surface, Mary adjusted quickly. An excellent student, she learned French and German and had an interest in politics. She was an attractive young girl, with clear skin and bright blue eyes. But she had a big problem: her mood could shift at the drop of a hat.

In 1839, Mary stumbled onto her chance at happiness. She was living with her sister in Illinois when she met a tall young lawyer at a dance. "Miss Todd," Abraham Lincoln supposedly said to her, "I want to dance with you in the worst way." Mary took the floor with him and never looked back.

Her family wasn't pleased with her new beau. Abraham was poor, socially awkward, and not as well educated as she was. But they had two things in common that were greater than money or class: idealism and political ambition. Mary wanted to wed a future President, and she was confident Abraham was one. Besides, she loved him. They married at her sister's house in November 1842.

At first, theirs was a contented life. Abraham built up his law practice and was elected to Congress. When he ran for President, Mary was deeply involved in his campaign. She was the first wife of a presidential candidate ever to attend rallies and to speak out against her husband's opponents. So united were they in their hopes for his career that when Abraham heard he'd won, he shouted to Mary, "We are elected!"

At forty-two, Mary found herself in the White House. It seemed she had everything she'd ever wanted—a successful husband, three lovely sons (a fourth had died young eleven years earlier), and national recognition. People thought her charming, well read, and intelligent. But it all went wrong fast.

Washington society looked down on short, plump Mary. Regardless of her education, they considered her a country bumpkin. Insecure Mary tried to prove them wrong by dressing in the height of fashion. But when her expensive gowns failed to change anyone's mind, an ever more anxious Mary spent greater and greater amounts on clothes. She didn't seem able to stop herself: in just four months, she bought three hundred pairs of lace gloves!

Mary's shopping sprees were a kind of sickness. They left the Lincolns in

Painting of the Lincoln family

tremendous debt. And they sparked even more criticism: many people felt Mary's extravagance was inappropriate in wartime, when so many Americans were suffering.

As if that weren't enough, some politicians spread rumors that Mary was a spy. After all, she was from a Southern state and her brothers were in the Confederate Army. It didn't matter that Mary had long opposed slavery and that perhaps her closest friend was a former slave. Abraham, gossips hinted, was forced to testify before Congress to defend her loyalty to the Union.

Thin-skinned Mary made a bad situation worse. She had jealous fits if Abraham spoke to other women. A person of extremes, she could be lovely one day, vicious the next, energetic in the morning, depressed by night.

But Abraham, who called her "Mother," knew the best of Mary. She was a keen judge of character who read the newspapers carefully and listened to congressional debates. Every night in their bedroom, they discussed the war, political strategy, and official appointments. She had a great memory for detail, and Abraham knew he could rely on her judgment.

In 1862, Mary suffered a tremendous blow. The Lincolns' eleven-year-old son, Willie, died of typhoid fever. He was the second child they'd lost to illness. Mary stayed in bed for days, so upset she couldn't go to the funeral. She never again entered the room in which Willie had passed away. Believing it was possible to contact the dead, she insisted that Willie's ghost came to visit her each night.

Tragedy continued to haunt her. In 1865, Abraham was assassinated just a week after the South surrendered. Mary was sitting right next to her husband when John Wilkes Booth fired the fatal shot. She was so grief-stricken that she couldn't leave her room for five weeks.

Now on her own, Mary was terrified of poverty. She had to find some way to pay her debts. But when she tried to raise money by selling her clothes, newspapers all over the country attacked her for being greedy. Even though she was the widow of a national hero, she herself was so unpopular that no one felt sympathy for her plight.

Her luck ran out completely in 1871. Tad, her eighteen-year-old son, died. For a while, Mary was so depressed she seemed to lose her mind. Thinking people were trying to poison her, she kept the lights on all night. She hid money away by sewing it into the lining of her dresses, yet at the same time spent huge amounts uncontrollably.

Finally, in 1875, Mary's only living son had a court declare her insane. The former First Lady was committed to an asylum. In despair, she tried to kill herself, but failed.

By 1876, Mary was released. It turned out an illness called diabetes, which was unknown at the time, might have been partly responsible for her behavior. But her life was now in ruins. She moved to France for several years, living in poverty in one small room. She returned to America in 1880, a wreck of a woman, her hair streaked with white, her face lined with wrinkles.

In her final years, Mary returned to her sister's home in Illinois. Paralyzed and unable to stand sunlight, she lived in a room where the shades were always down. Here, in the house in which she had married, where she'd begun what she hoped would be a life of glory, she died.

ELIZA McCARDLE JOHNSON

wife of the seventeenth President, Andrew Johnson

Born 1810, died 1876
First Lady 1865–1869

Andrew Johnson might never have been President if it hadn't been for Eliza Johnson. Like Abigail Fillmore, she gave her husband his start by teaching him everything she knew.

Eliza was born in Tennessee to a poor family. Her father was a shoemaker who died when she was very young. Like Abigail's mother, Eliza's was determined to give her an education. By making quilts and sandals, she earned enough money to send her blue-eyed girl to school.

When Eliza was sixteen, she met an eighteen-year-old tailor who had just arrived in town. Although Andrew Johnson's face was dirty from the dusty road, she instantly decided he was the man she would marry. And she did, one year later, in 1827.

Andrew had never been to school. Eliza immediately became his teacher.

She'd sit by his side and read aloud to him as he sewed. At night, she taught him reading, writing, math, geography, and history. To complete his education, she taught him how to speak properly. Although she herself wasn't interested in politics, she encouraged him to pursue a political career.

In 1842, Andrew was elected to Congress, and the Johnsons were prospering. Along with raising their five children, Eliza managed the money they had made from wise investments. The couple had come a long way.

Still, all was not well. By the time Andrew became Abraham Lincoln's Vice President, Eliza was sick with tuberculosis. When he inherited the Presidency after Abraham's murder, she felt she was too sick to be First Lady. It took thin, gray-haired, fifty-four-year-old Eliza four months to come to Washington. When

The impeachment trial of
Andrew Johnson

she finally arrived, she rarely left her room. With their daughter Martha acting as White House hostess, Eliza spent her time sewing, reading, and playing with her grandchildren.

But it wasn't just illness that kept Eliza in her room. Washington seemed to bring out her insecurities. The city itself frightened her—she'd been there only once before. Its social whirl made her feel inadequate. For years, she'd been close only to her family; now she feared she didn't have the proper social skills to be First Lady. Refusing all interviews, she said, ". . . I do not like this public life at all."

Behind the scenes, though, she was an immense help to Andrew. He was a temperamental man, and she knew just how to keep him calm. It was her job to keep track of what the magazines and newspapers reported and to cut out what he needed to read. So that he would sleep well at night, she gave him complimentary articles in the evening. Only during breakfast did she hand over the critical ones.

After the morning meal, the couple would discuss Andrew's upcoming meetings. In a sense, Eliza was still like his teacher. She was so well informed, Andrew treated her like a political adviser. One reporter said, "I should not wonder if Andrew Johnson did not consult his wife . . . more than he did any fellow statesman."

When his term was up, Eliza was delighted to leave Washington. She'd lived through his impeachment (Andrew was the first President accused by the House of Representatives of legal wrongdoing and sent for trial in the Senate, where he was acquitted). Now she was ready to return home. After seven restful years out of the spotlight, she died.

Portrait of Andrew Johnson

JULIA DENT GRANT

wife of the eighteenth President, Ulysses S. Grant

Born 1826, died 1902
First Lady 1869–1877

No one enjoyed being First Lady more than Julia Grant. Her years in the White House were marked by an extravagance and eye for luxury that not even Mary Lincoln could rival. Yet Americans loved Julia and enjoyed her excesses. It was a time called the "Gilded Age," and splurging was the style.

Julia had always led a comfortable life. A Missouri girl, she was born to a prosperous slave-owning family on a plantation called "Hardscrabble." Although her eyes were permanently crossed, she was a confident young woman, her father's favorite child. With a forceful personality that more than made up for her looks, she never lacked for suitors.

When she fell in love with Ulysses S. Grant (or "Ulys," as she called him), her family objected. He was a poor soldier without prospects who didn't earn enough to support her. But the young couple was determined. He called her "the lady of his dreams." Although his talents weren't obvious to most people, Julia had complete faith in Ulysses. The two married in 1848.

Their first years together were hard. Ulysses was forced out of the army for drinking too much, then had a tough time holding down a job. With four children to support, even optimistic Julia was frightened about their future. The Civil War saved them. The Union Army needed every man, and Ulysses was welcomed back. This time he came into his own, rising to Union commander and war hero, and then to the Presidency. Julia's faith in him had been rewarded.

So had her ambition. After Ulysses took the oath of office, he turned to her and lovingly said, "And now, my dear, I hope you're satisfied." She was.

Forty-three when she moved into the White House, Julia took full advantage of her husband's power and the money it attracted. It was as though she were bewitched by wealth. She had no ethical problem accepting gifts from rich backers, even though at times it looked as if Ulysses were being bought. Delighted by her fame and fortune, she adored being in Washington's limelight, socializing with the upper classes. If she wasn't out riding or dancing or watching a play, she was buying some expensive black satin gown that was the height of fashion. She had a particular fondness for high-priced jewels: diamonds were her favorite.

Nellie Grant's wedding took place in the East Room of the White House.

Julia's entertaining was famous for its excess. Dinner consisted of twenty-nine courses. She spared no expense when her daughter, Nellie, married in the White House. Nellie's dress cost $5,000, a fortune at the time. There were eight bridesmaids, two hundred guests, and presents that included a $500 handkerchief!

Instead of resenting Julia's wastefulness, most Americans enjoyed it. They believed she was fun-loving, not greedy. Her cheerfulness and energy made the country feel good about itself. People seemed happy to overlook her lapses. A stout, awkward woman, she was so forgetful she'd often wear just one earring or one glove. Her vision was so bad that she'd bump into people and furniture. Much more disturbing was the fact that she paid so little attention to the issues of the day. She once both endorsed and rejected the same congressional bill.

Julia was far from a well-informed First Lady. But she and Ulysses were so close that she influenced his decisions anyway. Interrupting him anytime she chose, she never hesitated to tell him her opinion. If he neglected to consult her about an appointment or an issue, she was insulted.

Throughout their White House years, the couple was rarely separated. Julia traveled with him, and they were openly affectionate. Ulysses often teased her, frequently calling her "Mrs. G."

Julia felt her years as First Lady were the happiest of her life. She urged Ulysses to run for a third term, and was keenly disappointed when he refused. When they moved out of the White House, she had to fight back tears.

Still, there were good times ahead. The Grants took a two-year around-the-world trip and were treated like celebrities, even by royalty. Upon their return, they moved to a mansion in New York paid for by wealthy friends. Ulysses's autobiography, written while he was dying of cancer, turned into a huge bestseller, earning a fortune. Julia wrote her own memoirs, which were not published until 1975.

In her later years, Julia came to believe strongly in the equality of women, supporting the campaign to win women the right to vote. But her life seemed empty after her husband's death in 1885. Seeking comfort, she returned to the place of her greatest happiness: Washington. It was there that she died at the age of seventy-seven.

Ulysses Grant, Union general and U.S. President

LUCY WARE WEBB HAYES

wife of the nineteenth President, Rutherford B. Hayes

Born 1831, died 1889
First Lady 1877–1881

Like Julia Grant, Lucy Hayes believed in women's rights. As a young woman she was firm in her convictions, but after her marriage to Rutherford B. Hayes, she seemed to give up all notion of female equality. In fact, she deliberately avoided most political issues once she was in the White House.

Her background had seemed to point her in a different direction. Lucy was born in Ohio to a family of abolitionists. Her father, a doctor, died when she was two, and her mother struggled to support her. But like Eliza Johnson, Lucy was lucky: her mother made sure she got a good education. Lucy would become the first First Lady to graduate from college.

As a student, Lucy was a feminist. She once said, "Woman's mind is as strong as man's . . . equal in all things and superior in some." She seemed convinced of her beliefs all the while Rutherford

courted her after their meeting at a college reception. Yet when they married in 1852, she put her beliefs aside and never looked back. Following his lead, she acted not as his intellectual partner but as a traditional wife and mother. Although she remained politically aware, attending congressional debates and taking up the cause of Civil War orphans, she rarely offered or was asked for her opinion and advice. One exception was abolition, on which Lucy's strong anti-slavery views influenced her husband.

Forty-five when she became First Lady, Lucy was devoted above all else to Rutherford. For her, devotion meant no disagreement. Though suffragists (those who supported the right of women to vote) expected her to speak out for their cause, she would not because Rutherford disagreed with them. Besides, under his influence she had herself begun to think

Lucy and Rutherford Hayes

every evening. Guests stood around and chatted. Liquor was never allowed.

This ban on liquor led some people to nickname her "Lemonade Lucy." They accused her of being straitlaced and dull. She certainly was proper. A religious woman, she held prayer meetings each morning and sang hymns with friends every Sunday night.

But most Americans didn't think Lucy was prissy. With her dark hair parted neatly in the center and pulled into a bun, she looked like a warm, kind person. She became so popular that reporters commented that she was "the most idolized woman in America."

Perhaps that's why Lucy traveled more than any First Lady before her. Constantly in the public eye, she made numerous appearances around the country and became the first widely photographed woman in the White House. Yet there was never any question about the center of her life: her husband. For their twenty-fifth wedding anniversary, she and Rutherford renewed their marriage vows. With her wearing her white satin wedding dress for the second time, they held a private ceremony in the White House with their five children around them.

After the couple left the White House, Lucy spent much of her time traveling, teaching Sunday school, and being active in her church. One day, while sewing, she had a stroke and died.

that women had to be better educated before getting the vote.

The changes in Lucy weren't due only to her marriage. The deaths of three children in infancy and her own health problems had affected her deeply. She'd become a woman who focused on simple pursuits. Her hobbies were fishing and gardening. In the White House, she concentrated on household concerns. Exploring its rooms, she found enough antique furniture and china to decorate it in proper historical style. She also modernized the building, introducing the first telephone.

She also provided a stark contrast to Julia Grant. Serious Lucy never wore jewelry and dressed simply but elegantly in dark long-sleeved dresses with high necks. She gave no gigantic state dinners, instead entertaining informally nearly

LUCRETIA (CRETE) RUDOLPH GARFIELD

wife of the twentieth President, James Garfield

Born 1832, died 1918
First Lady 1881

Like Lucy Hayes before her, young Crete Garfield had an independent mind but a husband who wanted her utter devotion. During the early years of their marriage, she and James Garfield often clashed. But over time, Crete adjusted to their life together and doted on her husband. The longer they were married, the more contented they became. But a bullet ended their happiness.

Crete and James met in college in Ohio. She had grown up on a farm and was raised by a religious family. A shy young woman, she had little social life until outgoing James came into her life. They courted for five years, mostly because he couldn't make up his mind if he wanted to marry her. Starting and stopping other relationships, he always returned to her. Finally, in 1858, they wed.

By this time, they were both school-teachers. Crete had grown used to earning her own money and controlling her life. Something of an intellectual, she knew Greek and Latin and had definite opinions of her own. But James expected to do the thinking for both of them.

Soon after the wedding, both of them realized they were miserable. So for the first four years of the marriage, they were together only about five months. In happier times later on, they looked back and called these the "years of darkness."

After James entered Congress in 1863, Crete confronted him about their separations. The couple started to spend more time together, reading, traveling, and living in the capital. They grew even closer after two of their children died (they had seven). Although it meant she had to keep her opinions to herself, Crete

Lithograph of the Garfield family

dedicated herself to his career, taking up the role of the good wife. While she insisted on time to herself every day, slowly she began to adopt James's view of the world.

She did not, however, accompany James to many social events. Though she was attractive, Washington society found the thin, whispery-voiced woman dull. She didn't mind. Just as she always had, she found parties boring, much preferring to study at the Library of Congress.

Crete was pleased with her husband's political success. Confident about his greatness, she was delighted with his nomination for the Presidency. But that didn't mean she was willing to become a public figure. She guarded her privacy all during the campaign, allowing just one photograph to be taken of her.

Yet Crete was the first First Lady to be pictured in a campaign: her face was featured on her husband's posters. It seemed fitting somehow that she played a role in his election, since by this time the couple was very close. When James won, she said, "It is a terrible responsibility to come to him and to me."

At forty-five, Crete moved into the White House. As ladylike as Lucy Hayes, she nonetheless reintroduced liquor

there. She was full of plans to redecorate the White House but fell ill with malaria just two months into James's term. The President hardly left her bedside, saying, "My thoughts center in her, in comparison with whom all else fades into insignificance." When she was well enough to travel, he took her to the New Jersey shore to complete her recovery.

On July 2, 1881, James was shot in the Washington train station on his way to visit his wife. As he was taken to the doctor, he told a friend, "Whatever happens, I want you to promise to look out for Crete." As soon as Crete heard the news, she returned home. Looking "frail, fatigued, desperate, but firm and quiet," according to one friend, she was still so weak from her illness that two men had to hold her up as she entered the White House. Once inside, however, she took charge of James's care, even preparing his food. When he died ten weeks later, Crete said, "Oh, why am I made to suffer this cruel wrong?"

In later years, she was a respected widow, admired by most Americans. To pass the time, she kept up her interest in the arts and constantly read. But until her death at age eighty-six, her energy was dedicated to preserving her husband's memory.

ELLEN (NELL) LEWIS HERNDON ARTHUR

wife of the twenty-first President, Chester A. Arthur

Born 1837, died 1880

Nell Arthur might have enjoyed being First Lady, but she never got the chance. She was dead by the time her husband, Chester A. Arthur, took office after James Garfield's assassination. After spending years resenting Chester's involvement in politics, she didn't get to enjoy its fruits.

Nell and Chester had their differences from the time they met. She was from a prominent slaveholding family in Virginia while he was a small-town Vermont boy. They met in New York when Nell came to visit her cousin, who was rooming with Chester. Almost instantly, they fell in love, and in 1859, they married.

Nell wasn't interested in politics. But she knew what she believed in—the South. The couple often argued during the Civil War, since he supported the Union while she backed the Confederacy.

Chester called Nell his "little rebel wife."

Even when the war ended, the disagreements didn't stop. By now a wealthy lawyer, Chester was often away on Republican Party business. While Nell shared his ambition, she felt lonely and left out. Her active social life no longer made up for Chester's absences.

In the early years of their marriage, Nell had enjoyed her role as Chester's gracious hostess. Lively and attractive, she'd made a point of dressing well. Yet she was no mere partygoer: she'd raised a lot of money for charity. She was also a devoted mother who'd always made time for her two children (a third died young).

But over time, she grew unhappy. Nell couldn't stand being neglected by the man she loved. As Chester considered running for Vice President, she thought about leaving him.

Yet it was neither neglect nor politics that killed her at age forty-two. It was her favorite pastime, singing. While waiting for her carriage after a benefit concert in New York City, Nell caught pneumonia, and she soon died. Chester—who had been busy with politics in Albany—was crushed. She had already fallen unconscious when he reached her side. He felt no one could replace her, saying, "Honors to me now are not what they once were."

Twenty months later, he was President. Although his youngest sister, Mary Arthur McElroy, helped him entertain, he had no official First Lady.

He kept a photograph of Nell in his bedroom, placing a rose in front of it every day. Chester's White House was, one woman said, "an abode of gloom."

Engraving of Chester A. Arthur

Mary Arthur McElroy, the President's sister, helped him entertain while he was in the White House.

FRANCES FOLSOM CLEVELAND PRESTON

wife of the twenty-second and twenty-fourth President, Grover Cleveland

Born 1864, died 1947
First Lady 1886–1889 and 1893–1897

Only twenty-one when she moved into the White House, Frances Cleveland was the youngest First Lady ever. Tall and pretty, she married Grover Cleveland in 1886, one year after he became President. To most Americans, their relationship was a complete surprise. He was twenty-seven years older than she was, and observers thought he'd been courting her mother. The two managed to keep their engagement secret and their wedding private.

The first President to be married in the White House, Grover himself planned the ceremony. He even decided on the vows that he and "Frank," as he called Frances, would take. On the day of the wedding, he had five wagonloads of flowers spread all through the White House. There were blossoms bursting from vases, lining mirrors, and filling up fireplaces. Frances wore a white satin gown with orange flower trim and a fifteen-foot-long train. Her jewelry was exquisite—a diamond necklace and a ring of diamonds and sapphires.

No reporters were allowed to attend the wedding. Only forty friends and relatives were present as the couple made their vows. They toasted each other with mineral water, since Frances disapproved of liquor. Afterward, church bells rang throughout the city, and a twenty-one-gun salute was fired.

Frances and Grover honeymooned in Maryland, and the press found them quickly. Reporters were so eager for news that they spied on the couple with binoculars. Throngs of people mobbed each of Frances's public appearances, anxious for a glimpse of her.

It was all quite a shock for the young

Grover and Frances Cleveland were married in the White House on June 2, 1886.

woman. After all, Frances had never expected to marry Grover. He was her father's law partner and friend, and had known her from the time of her birth in New York. In fact, it was Grover who'd bought her her first baby carriage! Frances's father died when she was eleven, and Uncle Cleve helped her mother raise her. She thought of him as her guardian, not as a future husband.

By the time Frances was a teenager, she was a confident young woman who seemed older than her years. With a good education behind her, she knew French, German, and Latin, played the piano, and was an amateur photographer. But while she was serious, rosy-cheeked Frances was far from glum. Her wonderful smile

matched her great sense of humor. With her wavy brown hair and blue eyes with long lashes, she was attractive and stylish. Once she went off to college, bachelor Grover realized he was in love with her.

The country was smitten, too. Americans hung photographs of her in their homes, while women imitated her hairstyle, the knot. Although they didn't have her permission, advertisers used her image to peddle their products. When Frances opened some White House receptions to the public, mobs of women jammed in to meet her. One day, nine thousand people stood in line just to shake her gloved hand. Tiring though they were, Frances wouldn't stop the receptions. She held them on Saturday afternoons so working women could come.

Frances and Grover were openly affectionate. But when he ran for reelection, Republicans spread the rumor that he got drunk and beat her. It wasn't true, but the lie helped defeat him. Still, Frances had a feeling about the future. When the Clevelands moved out of the White House, she told the staff, "We are coming back just four years from today."

And they did. Grover was the only President to be reelected after a loss. He won at least in part because Frances's picture appeared on his campaign posters.

Just as she had in Grover's first term, Frances stayed out of politics. She did believe strongly in one issue, though— equal education for women. But her attention was focused on more personal concerns: she gave birth to the first child born in the White House.

Though she was a new mother, Frances remained an active First Lady. Every Thursday, she gave a party for the entire Congress. She personally answered the thousands of letters she received from all over the country. Most important, she kept an eye on her husband. "She would watch over him," one member of the staff said, "as though he were one of the children."

When the Clevelands left the White House, Frances wept. She'd lived there so long it felt like home to her. Now she had five children to raise and a retired husband to look after. She and Grover led a happy life in Princeton, New Jersey, until his death in 1908. At just forty-four, Frances was a widow.

Nearly five years later, she wed a professor of archaeology, becoming the first presidential wife to marry after her husband's death. But to most Americans, she remained young Mrs. Cleveland.

Frances Cleveland's hairstyle, "the knot," was widely imitated.

CAROLINE (CARRIE) LAVINIA SCOTT HARRISON

wife of the twenty-third President, Benjamin Harrison

Born 1832, died 1892
First Lady 1889–1892

Without his wife, Carrie, Benjamin Harrison might never have been elected President. Easygoing and unpretentious, she was far more popular than he was. In contrast to her warmth, he was so distant and cold that he was known as the "human iceberg." Carrie knew how to melt him, though, and the two were very close.

Brown-eyed Carrie Scott met Benjamin in Ohio when she was just seventeen. Her father was both a minister and a teacher of science, and Benjamin was one of his students. The two shared a good education, sharp intelligence, and the same religious beliefs. Their church was so strict it forbade them to dance. Uptight Benjamin would never break the rule, but Carrie was too spirited to let it stop her. While Benjamin sat and watched, she danced with other men.

Talented in both music and art, she was creative and energetic.

Still, the two fell deeply in love. They became engaged but kept it secret because he couldn't yet support her. They were living in different cities; Benjamin studied law, while Carrie taught music. They missed each other terribly. Anxious to get her letters, Benjamin went to the local post office so often that the clerks used to laugh when they saw him. Carrie suffered even more, actually falling ill. They finally married in 1853.

Their first years together were difficult. Money was so tight that they had to borrow to buy food. But Benjamin worked very hard and built a successful career. His law practice flourished, and he became politically involved. The couple paid a price for their good fortune, though—Benjamin was so often at the

Caroline Harrison and her family

office he was hardly ever home. Alone with two children, a neglected Carrie became deeply unhappy.

The Civil War, oddly enough, helped save the Harrisons' marriage. Away from his family, with death all around him on the battlefield, soldier Benjamin realized Carrie was the most important part of his life. He wrote her a passionate letter promising never to slight her again.

Carrie was thrilled.

After the war, Benjamin's political career took off and he was eventually elected to the Senate. But he kept his promise and was careful always to spend time with his wife. When the Republican Party nominated him for President, he had Carrie's full support. It turned out to be vital, since the party wanted to involve her in his campaign. Carrie's cheery presence was needed to soften Benjamin's coldness.

It was a time, though, when most Americans felt women shouldn't be active in politics. So the Harrisons ran what was called a "front-porch campaign." Carrie didn't travel with Benjamin or make political speeches. Instead, voters came to their house when he was home, and she greeted them on the front porch. Over 300,000 people met the Harrisons this way. Carrie became a national figure.

She was fifty-six when she became First Lady. Despite poor health, she brought her usual gusto to the job. Almost immediately, she made dramatic changes in the way the White House was run. Called the best housekeeper among all presidential wives, Carrie modernized the building. Stylish clothing didn't interest her—she was too busy supervising the installation of a new kitchen and bathrooms. She filled the rooms with plants and flowers, among them orchids she herself raised. She started the famous White House china collection, even painting her own pattern for her dishes.

Carrie introduced electric lights to the White House, but that didn't mean she made good use of them. She and Benjamin were so frightened of getting an electric shock that they'd sleep with the lights on rather than touch the switches.

When she wasn't busy running the White House, one issue consistently grabbed Carrie's attention: the inequality of women's education. On the condition that female students be admitted, she helped raise money for the Johns Hopkins University School of Medicine in Baltimore.

Photograph of Benjamin Harrison

As Benjamin's term went on, Carrie got physically weaker and weaker. By 1892, it was clear she had tuberculosis and was dying. Although Benjamin was campaigning for reelection, he limited his appearances. He was at her bedside when she died at the age of sixty. He lost the election, perhaps in part because she wasn't there to help.

IDA SAXTON McKINLEY

wife of the twenty-fifth President, William McKinley

Born 1847, died 1907
First Lady 1897–1901

Poor Ida McKinley was sick the entire time she lived in the White House. From the moment she collapsed at the inaugural ball to the day she left Washington to start a new life, Americans knew her as frail, nervous, and ill.

She wasn't always that way. Born in Ohio to a well-to-do family, Ida was a bright, lively young woman. She had the courage to be different: unlike most women of her class, she worked for a living. Her banker father believed she should learn to take care of herself, and Ida agreed. So, instead of attending college, she got a job as a bank teller. She enjoyed the work, even learning about finance from her father.

Short and dark, with blue eyes, Ida had many interests outside the bank. She loved music, knitting, and playing cards. Her energy, and her wealth, attracted many suitors. But she was interested in

just one: William McKinley, a lawyer, whom she met at a picnic when she was twenty-two. He courted her in part by visiting her at the bank. Quickly devoted to each other, they married in 1871. He nicknamed her "Dearest," and she called him "The Major" or "My Precious."

Their happiness was short-lived. First Ida's mother died. A year later, so did their two daughters. Then Ida's health failed. Some people thought she'd had a nervous breakdown, but it is likely she was stricken with epilepsy. Though decades had passed since Elizabeth Monroe suffered from the same illness, doctors still didn't know much about it. Most Americans so feared the disease that the McKinleys never discussed the cause of her condition.

Between painful headaches and fainting spells, Ida often had seizures. These made her not only ill but also depressed.

As her husband became a congressman and then governor of Ohio, her sickness worsened and the medicines she took intensified her depression. Yet she supported his career, and they remained close.

William was a doting husband. Even in the middle of a political crisis, he always made time for her. They ate all their meals together. If he had to go away on business, he wrote her faithfully once a day. He even let her win at cards.

It was lucky for Ida that he was so caring. More than any medication, she needed William's attention. She wouldn't make decisions without getting his opinion, even interrupting his meetings to ask if he liked her dress. Although she had trouble walking, she insisted on accompanying him on trips. No matter what her condition, she never skipped a social engagement if he was also invited.

When William became President, Ida tried her best to perform her duties as First Lady. The pale forty-nine-year-old would greet guests at White House receptions propped up by pillows in an armchair. Dressed in beautiful, lacy gowns and adorned with diamonds, she'd attend dinners no matter how ill she felt. Sometimes a seizure would hit her in the middle of a sentence. With the muscles in her face twisting, she'd suddenly black out. William would cover her face with a napkin or his white silk handkerchief until the seizure passed. Then Ida would continue with what she'd been saying as though nothing had happened.

Many people in Washington were impressed by William's devotion to Ida. Some thought he was close to a saint. Voters seemed to agree on his virtues—they reelected him in 1900. But the following year, he was shot by an assassin. Even as he lay dying, Ida was in his thoughts. He moaned, "My wife, be careful how you tell her—oh, be careful!"

Ida surprised everyone with her strength. She rushed to William's side and tried to raise his spirits. But after eight days of struggle, he died. Crushed, she commented, "Life to me is dark now."

Yet all of a sudden, her illness disappeared. She lived another six years, moving back to Ohio to be with her sister. It was reported that she never had another seizure.

President and Mrs. McKinley at a dinner party

EDITH (EDIE) KERMIT CAROW ROOSEVELT

wife of the twenty-sixth President, Theodore Roosevelt

Born 1861, died 1948
First Lady 1901–1909

Edith Roosevelt was an intensely private woman who married a very public man. That wasn't the only contradiction in her life. Born into high society, she was a social snob who followed strict rules of behavior, yet she was the mother of one of the most informal, fun-loving families ever to occupy the White House. While Edie, as she was called, kept her distance from both the press and the voters, she was very involved with her husband's career. She may have appeared removed from events, but she knew everything that was happening in Washington.

The contradictions started with her marriage. The man she called Theodore (and not Teddy, as many people did) was her opposite. She was sensible and reserved, whereas he was impulsive and high-spirited. Edie would have preferred to wed a quiet family man, not a politician; but from childhood on, she was hopelessly in love with Theodore Roosevelt. They'd practically grown up together in New York, where their wealthy families were close. Theodore's sister was Edie's best friend. From the time they were teenagers, the two planned to marry.

When Theodore left to go to college, Edie waited for him at home. But he didn't return—he fell in love with another woman and married her. Edie was crushed.

But Theodore's wife died while giving birth to their first child. A year and a half later, Edie and Theodore bumped into each other by accident. Their love was rekindled. In 1886, they married, and over the years, they had five children together. Edie raised his daughter by his first wife as though she were her own.

Theodore Roosevelt and family as they appeared when they lived in the White House

From the start, Edie discouraged Theodore from pursuing a political career, believing he should devote himself to his family. But Theodore didn't listen. By 1901, he'd been elected Vice President. After McKinley's assassination, he was President. At forty, elegant, auburn-haired Edie was First Lady.

This "life of confinement," as she called it, wasn't what she wanted. But she didn't hesitate to do her duty. Immediately taking over the White House, she managed its housekeeping down to every detail. She was one of the most organized First Ladies ever. Despite this, by 1902 she was overwhelmed by work. So she hired a social secretary, the first First Lady to do so.

Always wary of the spotlight, Edie nonetheless made the White House the center of Washington society. She entertained constantly. However, she rarely invited those not of her own class and race. If people arrived whom she didn't like, she'd pretend to have a headache to avoid them.

Her social events often served a larger purpose. Since prim and proper Edie wanted no scandal to touch her husband's administration, she did her best to keep up with gossip about those around him. What better way to do that than at her many receptions and teas, and at her weekly meetings with the wives of cabinet officials?

Edie craved privacy, but she also had a public vision for the White House: she wanted it to be the cultural heart of America. That's why she made sure there were weekly concerts by the most prominent musicians in the world. With her sense of history and art, she created a special gallery to hold portraits of every First Lady, including her own.

Even more important, she recognized the need to preserve and restore the White House. She was the first First Lady to see it as part of the national heritage, a museum for all Americans. Not only did she prevent the sale of historical items, she also tried to reacquire some of the original furnishings that had been sold.

No First Lady respected history more than Edie. But she also felt the White House should be a comfortable place to live. Under her direction, the building was renovated. The West Wing was added, separating the rooms in which the President worked from those in which he and his family lived. Finally, the First Family had a space of its own.

That pleased Edie. More than anything else, she wanted privacy. She rarely granted interviews and kept her children away from the press. She once wrote, "One hates to feel that all one's life is public property." Standing straight as a board in the middle of social gatherings, she was so wary of people that she'd clutch a bouquet so that she didn't have to shake hands.

Edie was something of a loner. Her emotions, she felt, belonged to her and her alone. The only person she was truly close to was Theodore. Even those she loved she kept her distance from. As one friend commented, "You could live in the same room with Edith for fifty years, and never know what she was really thinking."

Her standoffishness didn't stem from shyness. Edie was so confident she never worried about her appearance. But her view of herself wasn't always accurate.

She considered herself strictly a wife and mother, yet she had a keen grasp of politics and much influence on her husband. Clearly, she had a mind of her own, yet she believed women should not be independent of men.

She went out of her way to make sure the center of her life was her family. No matter how busy her days were, she always spent time with her husband and children. They needed her: a wild bunch, they were loud and energetic, relying on her to be the disciplinarian. The President himself seemed to her so much like a child that she called him "my fifth boy" and kept him on an allowance.

Yet they were genuine partners. Every day, Edie rose at dawn and strolled through the gardens with Theodore, even if it was raining. Every night, they discussed the day's events. Theodore valued her advice so much that he made time between appointments to consult her. An avid reader, she pored over newspapers and marked articles for him to look at.

After two terms in office, Edie had had enough. But Theodore still wanted to be President. Four years after they'd left the White House, he ran for the Republican nomination again. Edie heartily disapproved. When he lost, she said, "You cannot know how happy I am that the White House is not ahead of us."

Theodore died twenty-nine years before she did, yet Edie never remarried. Leading a quiet life, she devoted most of her time to travel, charity work, and her family. As death neared, she was still determined to maintain her privacy. She destroyed all of Theodore's letters to her, along with many personal files. Even after she was gone, she didn't want people to know her secrets.

HELEN (NELLIE) HERRON TAFT

wife of the twenty-seventh President, William Howard Taft

Born 1861, died 1943
First Lady 1909–1913

No one wanted to be First Lady more than ambitious, intelligent Nellie Taft. As a young woman, she at first planned to make her own way to the top, but quickly realized that most careers were off limits because of her sex. Besides, she also wanted a husband and family and feared independence would cost her the opportunity. So Nellie came up with the perfect solution: wed a man who would succeed. That man turned out to be William Howard Taft.

From the start, Nellie seemed meant for power. Her father was a prominent lawyer whose former partner was Rutherford B. Hayes. She herself was an excellent student in love with music and books. When she was seventeen, Nellie had an experience that set her on her path: she visited President Hayes in the White House. After that, she was determined to leave Ohio, and on the arm of a future President.

She didn't have long to wait. When Nellie was eighteen, she met William Howard Taft, a lawyer, at a party. They got to know each other over the next few years, in part at book discussions that she and her friends organized on Saturday nights. But while William was falling in love with pretty, brown-haired Nellie, her schoolteaching job was depressing her more and more. Sometimes, she'd sit and cry for hours.

There was another reason she was upset. Smart and attractive though she was, Nellie wasn't confident that William truly cared for her. She was so insecure about his love that he had to propose three times before she agreed to marry him. At last, in 1886, they wed.

Over the next few years, William became a judge and then a diplomat.

Nellie knew he had the makings of a successful politician, but William himself was far less ambitious. More than anything, he wanted to be appointed to the Supreme Court. But Nellie had her eye on the Presidency. As William said, she was "the politician in the family."

She pushed and prodded her easygoing husband to achieve her goal. "I want you in line for the presidential nomination," she stated. So that he could accept political appointments that furthered his

President Taft surrounded by his family

career, she moved the family (there were three children) every few years.

By the time William was nominated for President, Nellie's ambition was so strong it made her anxious. The closer William got to the top, the more she worried. In contrast to her calm, steady husband, she was nervous about everything. Some people nicknamed her "Nervous Nellie."

When she was forty-seven, Nellie's longtime wish was fulfilled. She happily admitted to reporters, "It has always been my ambition to see Mr. Taft President of the United States. . . ." On Inauguration Day, she became the first First Lady to ride with her husband in a carriage back to the White House.

It was a sign of her influence to come. Although the Tafts kept it hidden, Nellie had tremendous sway over William's policies. She joined in political debates and helped decide on cabinet and diplomatic appointments. No one she disliked was nominated to a post. Although she stated, "I confess only to a lively interest in my husband's work . . . ," in reality, William never made a decision without consulting her. He once wrote on a memo, "Memorandum for Mrs. Taft—the real president. . . ."

The couple was so good at keeping Nellie's role secret that few people believed she took any interest in politics. They had no idea that William had a poor memory and relied on his wife to remind him of names, faces, and facts. Nellie was so convinced voters would disapprove if they knew of her influence that she disguised it, saying, "I do not believe in a woman meddling in politics. . . ."

She ran the White House as well. No detail escaped her attention. At her insistence, certain rooms were closed to tourists. She allowed no one on the staff

to wear a beard or mustache. She insisted that the President ride in a car and not the traditional horse and carriage. So that the family could have fresh milk, she got a cow and let it graze on the White House lawn. It was she who brought the three thousand Japanese cherry trees to Washington that are now celebrated in the annual Cherry Blossom Festival.

But in May 1909, whirlwind Nellie collapsed on the presidential yacht. She'd had a stroke and couldn't speak or move her right side.

Slowly, she recovered. Her mind was keen—the problem was her body. William spent hours each day at her bedside, reading to her and helping her learn to speak again. Determined not to lose control, she continued to plan state dinners. Since she wasn't well enough to attend, she'd eat alone in a nearby room to overhear the conversation.

William was not reelected. Nellie was so upset she couldn't say good-bye to the White House staff. Yet it turned out that she didn't miss being First Lady as much as she had feared. The couple spent time in Connecticut, where William taught law at Yale. Then in 1921, to the Tafts' delight, William was appointed Chief Justice and they returned to the center of the capital's political and social life.

Keeping up her political interests, Nellie supported immigration rights, women's suffrage, and higher education for women. In 1914, she became the first First Lady to publish her memoirs. Nellie had had a dream at seventeen and made it come true.

ELLEN LOUISE AXSON WILSON

first wife of the twenty-eighth President, Woodrow Wilson

Born 1860, died 1914
First Lady 1913–1914

Ellen Wilson always seemed to sacrifice her desires for the sake of her loved ones. First, she put aside her own career ambitions to care for her motherless brothers and sister. Then there was Woodrow Wilson.

Raised in a small Georgia town, Ellen was the oldest daughter of a minister whose family owned slaves before the Civil War. Brilliant and artistically gifted, she was different from the other girls in town. From adolescence, she had a dream: to leave the South and study art in New York City. But when her mother died while Ellen was in college, she stayed in Georgia to help raise her brothers and sister.

A few years later, young lawyer Woodrow Wilson spotted rosy-cheeked Ellen in church. He immediately decided he was going to marry her. But Ellen had other ideas. Her siblings were old enough now for her to leave them. More committed to her dream than to marriage, she left Georgia to take art classes in New York.

It was a thrilling time for Ellen. Although such behavior was frowned upon in women, she went to lectures on her own, soaking up the latest artistic and political theories. She read radical publications, painted nudes, and exhibited her work. Excited by the world of ideas around her, she was far more fascinated by books than by fashion.

For his part, Woodrow continued to pursue her. He had given up the law to become a professor of history. They wrote to each other every day. Ellen began to fall in love with him. He seemed to agree with her that the best marriage was one between equals.

At last, she consented to marry, and the two wed in 1885. But it soon became clear that Woodrow wanted a traditional wife. Putting his needs first, Ellen sacrificed her artistic career.

By the time Woodrow became president of Princeton University, Ellen's dream had faded. Although she continued to paint and occasionally exhibit, she spent most of her time raising their three daughters and helping him write speeches and lectures. When he had an administrative problem, it was usually her idea that solved it.

Ellen didn't mind—by now, she worshiped Woodrow. She was happy with their life at the university. But when Woodrow abandoned academic life to become governor of New Jersey, Ellen was miserable. She didn't want him to run for President, yet typically gave in to his wishes. Helping out in his campaign, she made public appearances at his side.

But Ellen remained depressed. When he was elected, she commented, "I am naturally the most unambitious of women and life in the White House has

The Wilson family in 1912, in the backyard of the New Jersey governor's mansion

no attractions for me." The day before the inauguration, she burst into tears. Shy and insecure, she didn't think she could handle the responsibility of being First Lady.

Once she was in the White House, however, fifty-two-year-old Ellen found she loved the job. Right away, she filled the family's living quarters with various works of art. She resumed her painting and helped sponsor exhibits of women's crafts.

She also developed an interest in politics. While she didn't have much influence over Woodrow's policies, she was not entirely without clout: he so trusted her judgments of people that she had a say in his appointments. He also relied on her help with his speeches.

Ellen was a gracious hostess who had no trouble fulfilling her social role. But she felt a First Lady should do more. She tried to speak out on public issues. Though she would not publicly support the suffrage movement in which she believed, she took up the cause of improved working conditions for government employees. At that time, women workers didn't even have an on-the-job bathroom they could use, and Ellen made sure they got one.

Her old independence of spirit resurfaced as she became determined to clean up the slums. Soon after Woodrow's inauguration, she took members of Congress on a tour of a poor neighborhood—urging them to pass legislation she thought would help. But when the bill became law, buildings were knocked down and not replaced, and people found themselves homeless.

Unfortunately, Ellen wasn't around to help. By the time the bill went through, over a year had passed and Ellen was

Photograph of Woodrow Wilson

dead. Bright's disease, which affected her kidneys, had killed her.

While she'd lain ill in the White House, Woodrow wouldn't leave her room. He did all his work at her bedside. True to form, her last thoughts were of him. She asked her doctor, "Promise me that you will take good care of Woodrow."

As she passed away, Woodrow held her hand, then burst into tears. Finally, he cried out, "Oh my God, what am I going to do?" For two nights, he didn't budge from her body. Weeks went by as he roamed through the White House as if he were lost. His soft-voiced Ellen was gone.

EDITH BOLLING GALT WILSON

second wife of Woodrow Wilson

Born 1872, died 1961
First Lady 1915–1921

Unlike Ellen Wilson, Woodrow Wilson's second wife, Edith Wilson, had no interest in politics. Yet it was she who ended up with more power than any other First Lady. The President became seriously ill during his second term, and Edith came close to running the country—or at least, that's what was rumored. Historians suspect she covered up just how disabled Woodrow was so that he wouldn't be removed from office: she feared he'd die if he was replaced. A loyal wife and a stubborn, determined woman, Edith grabbed the reins of power to save her husband's life and keep him in office.

She may have been the secret head of state, but she didn't believe in the equality of the sexes. She opposed granting women the right to vote. From childhood on, Edith felt a woman could succeed only if she married well.

Born in Virginia, Edith was one of eleven children. She claimed to be related to Pocahontas. Her father was a judge, but the family had little money to spare. Educated at home by her father and grandmother, she never learned to write properly.

At the age of twenty-four, Edith left her family and married a prosperous jeweler. But by the time he died twelve years later, his business was close to ruin. Edith took it over, learning to make decisions without worrying what people thought. Her confidence rose as the business boomed. She enjoyed her success, living and dressing well.

In 1915, Edith met Woodrow Wilson through a friend of hers, his cousin. Ellen had been dead just seven months, but Woodrow was lonely. He was instantly attracted to the stylish Edith, courting her in secret and sending her passionate love letters.

By the end of 1915, they were married.

In some ways, Edith and Woodrow were an odd match. He was an intellectual and the most powerful politician in the land. She was so uninterested in public affairs she didn't even know who'd run for President in the last election. He put his faith in reason, while she believed in astrology.

Yet they were deeply in love. He called her "his heart's companion." They were such a close couple he consulted her on many issues despite her ignorance of politics, even confiding top-secret information such as wartime codes. Actually sitting with Woodrow in his office as he worked, forty-three-year-old Edith didn't hesitate to offer him her opinions. So unwilling were they to separate that she became the first First Lady to accompany her husband on diplomatic trips abroad. Then, in September 1919, Woodrow had a stroke. It left him paralyzed and blind on his left side, his voice no more than a whisper. He was so sick that he couldn't leave the bed. To keep the nation from realizing the extent of his illness, Edith hid him from view. Overnight, the most powerful man in America simply disappeared. It was the start of what Edith called her "stewardship," when she was the single link between the President and the world.

She permitted only his doctors to see him. If cabinet members and government officials had questions, they had to come to her for answers. She read all documents intended for the President, and determined what was important. But she denied making any judgments on her own, insisting that she discussed the issues with Woodrow and merely announced his decisions.

Both Congress and the country were uncomfortable with the situation. No one was able to tell if it was the President who was running the government, or Edith. Soon there was an outcry. The press called her "Acting First Man." One senator said, "We have a Petticoat government! Mrs. Wilson is President!" She was labeled everything from "Iron Queen" to "Acting Ruler" to the "Presidentress of the United States." But she didn't care. She said, "I am not thinking of the country now, I am thinking of my husband."

By the spring of 1920, Woodrow was well enough to resume his responsibilities. He even considered running for a third term until Edith forbade it. When he died in 1924, a grieving Edith went into seclusion for a year. When she rejoined Washington society, she dedicated her life to keeping his memory alive. Although she survived him by thirty-eight years, she never remarried. She died at eighty-nine—on Woodrow's birthday.

President and Mrs. Wilson

FLORENCE KLING HARDING

wife of the twenty-ninth President, Warren G. Harding

Born 1860, died 1924
First Lady 1921–1923

Florence Harding craved the kind of power Edith Wilson had. Intelligent and strong-willed, she was a lot like Nellie Taft—a tremendously ambitious woman who pushed a less ambitious man into the Presidency. In a sense, Florence was more devoted to Warren G. Harding's career than he was. While he pursued his love of a good time, she tended to his image and made sure he practiced smart politics.

Yet Florence had once been as wild as Warren. Born in Ohio, she was the daughter of a hardware store owner who became the richest man in town. Frustrated that she wasn't a boy, her father disapproved of nearly everything she did. Florence became a rebel. By the time she got to the Cincinnati Conservatory of Music, she was hanging out with a noisy, fun-loving crowd. At nineteen, she suddenly married a young

man named Henry De Wolfe: she was pregnant, and in those days, society shunned single mothers.

The marriage was doomed from the start. Henry drank too much and was a business failure. He deserted the family when their son was just two. Florence returned home, but while her father adopted the boy, he refused to take her in. She ended up supporting herself by giving piano lessons. In 1886, she and Henry divorced.

Florence was still giving lessons when she met Warren Harding, the local newspaper editor, five years her junior. He was handsome and charming, and Florence fell in love. Her father opposed the match, even threatening to shoot Warren. The two married anyway in 1891, and Mr. Kling didn't talk to Florence for seven years. Fifteen years passed before he would visit the couple. (When Mr. Kling finally met Warren, he found that he liked him!)

By that time, Warren was an influential man, in part because of his wife's talent. She had helped him build his newspaper into a leading Republican voice in the state. "I went down there," she said, "intending to help out for a few days and I stayed fourteen years." The couple had no children, and Florence could throw herself into her work. Still, she was a devoted wife who made her husband's lunch every day.

When Warren ran for political office, well-informed Florence became heavily involved. She said, "I have only one real hobby—it's my husband." To Warren, she was like a mother—someone who, no matter what, took care of him. They had an unspoken agreement: he listened to her political advice, and she turned a blind eye to his relationships with other women. Despite his poor health, he agreed to run for President in part because he knew how much she wanted to be First Lady.

Although she was ill (she had just one functioning kidney), Florence helped

President and Mrs. Harding departing on a trip to Alaska

manage Warren's campaign. She developed the original strategy of appealing to women. It was the first election in which women would cast ballots, and Florence realized they could swing the vote.

During the campaign, Florence visited an astrologer. To her great joy, the astrologer predicted Warren would win. But she followed with a gloomy forecast: Warren would die in office, and Florence would follow soon after.

When Warren indeed won, Florence felt great pride. She began to call herself a "President-maker" and "President-ruler." A depressed Warren told her, "I have lost my freedom," but her only response was, "Well, Warren, I have got you the Presidency. What are you going to do with it?"

At sixty-one, Florence was First Lady. Self-conscious about her age and health, she went to the hairdresser every day. Dressed stylishly in blue to match her eyes, she wore makeup to look younger. It worked. Although, in 1922, she was so ill she spent six months in bed, most people thought she was much younger than she was.

Her natural friendliness placed her front and center with the voters. She was the first First Lady to make public speeches and meet with the press. Often describing herself as "just plain folks," she sometimes guided tourists through White House rooms. She was so eager to please that she once shook seven thousand hands at a reception. When Girl Scout troops came visiting, she greeted them in her own Girl Scout uniform. Through it all, she was guarded by the Secret Service, the first First Lady to receive such protection.

Florence was an effective hostess, but she spent most of her time on politics. As one of Warren's major advisers, she often wrote or edited his speeches. She herself believed in women's rights and animal rights, and was passionate about helping World War I veterans. She received so much mail that the White House staff had to help her respond.

At times, it seemed Florence was more interested in governing than Warren was. He seemed to sit back and let her take over. Nicknamed "the Duchess" by her husband, she bragged, "I know what's best for the President; I put him in the White House." As for Warren, he'd often say, "I'll have to check with the Duchess," before making a decision.

Yet he was capable of calling his own shots and sometimes resented her for issuing orders. They often argued, and Florence felt unappreciated. Perhaps if he *had* let her make his appointments, he would have avoided the scandal that made them both despair. It turned out that a number of Warren's cabinet members and associates were crooks who took bribes.

In 1923, Warren died suddenly of a blood clot while Florence was reading him the newspaper. The night before the funeral, she sat still and silent by the coffin, finally placing a bouquet of flowers on it. Then she murmured, "No one can hurt you now, Warren."

As a vicious rumor spread through Washington that she had poisoned her husband, Florence went home to Ohio. Fussing over Warren's image to the last, she burned many of his White House papers, fearing that they would be used to embarrass him.

A year and three months later, she, too, died. It had turned out that the astrologer was right.

GRACE ANNA GOODHUE COOLIDGE

wife of the thirtieth President, Calvin Coolidge

Born 1879, died 1957
First Lady 1923–1929

Not many people understood why Grace Goodhue married Calvin Coolidge. After all, he was a gruff man of few words, while she was a woman who loved a good time. Grace's mother certainly objected to the match. She thought her charming, intelligent daughter could do better than spend her life with a sourpuss Republican lawyer. When Calvin asked for Grace's hand, Mrs. Goodhue said her daughter wasn't ready for marriage. Grace, she told him, couldn't even bake bread. But Calvin wouldn't be put off. "I can *buy* bread," he replied. When he told Grace, "I am going to be married to you," Grace agreed.

Calvin made a good choice. Grace was a University of Vermont graduate—the first First Lady to get her degree from a coed school. Attractive, with wavy black hair and hazel eyes, she was outgoing and popular. One of her favorite pastimes was dancing, and she never lacked for partners. She had a serious side, too—for four years, she was a dedicated teacher of the deaf.

When Grace married Calvin, she gave up her career and her active social life. Calvin wanted a traditional wife, and Grace agreed. She learned quickly that his concerns came first: during their 1905 honeymoon, Calvin suddenly left her to campaign for a local Massachusetts office.

Calvin didn't allow Grace to participate actively in his political success. From the first, the couple agreed to keep his career separate from family life. He never asked Grace for her opinion or consulted her on issues. Years passed before she even heard him make a speech. He was so intent on keeping her out of politics that they ended up spending most of their

President and Mrs. Coolidge walk on the lawn of the newly decorated White House.

time apart. During the week, she was a single mother, raising their two sons and caring for the house on her own. Calvin came home from the state capital only on weekends.

Grace's life was hard. Calvin was extremely thrifty. Even after he was elected governor of Massachusetts, she had no phone, no household help, and no electricity. There was one thing he was generous about, however—Grace's wardrobe. Calvin wanted his wife to be a fashion plate and never wear the same party dress twice. Although Grace wore

little makeup and no jewelry, her gowns were always stunning.

When Calvin was elected Vice President, Grace became increasingly important to his success. That was because everybody liked her, including his enemies. Warm and friendly, with a great sense of humor, she could make even strangers feel comfortable. It was she who eased his way into Washington social life. While "Silent Cal," as he was called, rarely spoke at dinners, Grace was known as a "champion smiler."

After Warren Harding's death, Calvin

became President. Forty-four-year-old Grace found herself First Lady. Soon after, tragedy struck as the couple's teenage son suddenly died. Grace was slow to recover from her grief, but when she did, she made White House parties fun again. With her taste and style, she helped shape 1920s fashion, introducing red as a popular color for clothes.

The public loved her. Politicians did, too. She was a glamorous woman who was also down-to-earth. Whistling and singing to the radio or phonograph, she typed her own letters, dusted furniture, and gardened in the White House grounds. When she was upset or angry, she didn't scream—she knitted. An athlete, she kept herself fit and rooted loudly for the Boston Red Sox. In Washington, she was often seen walking her two beloved white collies, accompanied by a Secret Service agent.

The White House staff liked her so much that they nicknamed her "Sunshine." Calvin himself was proud of her, particularly about how well she handled people. He said, "I don't know what I would do without her."

He meant it. Calvin needed Grace around him all the time. While he rarely showed it in public, Grace knew he loved her. She wrote to him every day whenever she was away, and he was so anxious to get her letters that he'd go downstairs to the White House mailroom himself.

Still, Calvin kept Grace in the dark about his administration. Often, she found out about his political decisions from the press. He had rules she was expected to follow so that she'd never embarrass him politically. That was why she never expressed an opinion in public or engaged in gossip. She didn't dance, drive a car, ride a horse, or smoke. Because Calvin didn't want her to make even a single speech, she used sign language when reporters demanded she address them.

No matter how ridiculous the rules seemed to outsiders, Grace never questioned them. It didn't even bother her when Calvin announced he wasn't running for reelection without mentioning it to her first. She declared, "I am rather proud of the fact that after nearly a quarter of a century of marriage my husband feels free to make his decisions and act on them without consulting me. . . ."

Privately, Grace was delighted that Calvin's career was over. She was tired of the spotlight and the burdens of her hostessing role. When Calvin resumed practicing law, Grace did volunteer work with the deaf and wrote poetry.

After his death, she became her own person. Turning down a proposal of marriage, she cut her hair, traveled, and spoke out whenever she wanted. She missed Calvin, though, telling a friend, "I am just a lost soul. Nobody is going to believe how I miss being told what to do." She had another twenty-five years of making her own decisions before she, too, passed away.

Photograph of Calvin Coolidge

LOU HENRY HOOVER

wife of the thirty-first President, Herbert Hoover

Born 1874, died 1944
First Lady 1929–1933

Lou Hoover is remembered as the wife of the man blamed for the Great Depression, a period when millions of Americans were without work and desperately poor. Yet if it hadn't been for that catastrophe, she'd be recalled as one of the most cultured, well-traveled women of her time. She was also a true adventurer. She had to be. In the early years of her marriage to the man she called "Bertie," he hopped from engineering job to engineering job around the world. Lou found herself in distant, even dangerous places. She loved the excitement. No matter what Herbert Hoover did, or where he went, she followed, sharing his concerns and helping in his work. Their marriage was a true partnership that lasted through the White House years.

The two met at Stanford University in 1894. Lou, the only female geology student, was introduced to Herbert in the lab. At first glance, they seemed ill matched. She'd had a privileged childhood—her father was a banker—while shy Herbert was poor and an orphan. Lou excelled at sports and was an excellent rider. Herbert wasn't particularly athletic and didn't like horses. But they were both Iowa-born and California-raised. They loved to hike and camp and collect rocks. Herbert sensed that Lou was the woman for him.

When he graduated, he went off to work in Australia, careful to keep in touch with Lou. She finished college and became the first American woman to get a geology degree. But she couldn't find a job in the field—no one wanted to hire a woman. So she ended up teaching in a public school. One day, a telegram arrived for her. It was from Herbert, asking her to marry him. She wired back one word: yes.

In 1899, they wed and left immediately for China. Herbert had a new job there searching for minerals. From the very first, Lou accompanied him on his expeditions. Traveling by boat, pony, mule, and oxcart, they had to be protected from bandits by armed bodyguards. Lou learned Chinese—one of seven languages she spoke.

Then suddenly the Chinese took up arms against foreigners. It was the Boxer Rebellion, and shots whizzed through the Hoovers' house. Lou wasn't cowed. While bombs fell outside, she played solitaire to pass the time. Each day, she bicycled through a hail of bullets to the hospital, where she helped nurse the wounded. She even learned how to use a gun.

Finally, Lou and Herbert left China. But their life didn't calm down. Herbert established a successful mining engineering business, and the couple found themselves traveling through Europe, Egypt, Japan, and India, among other places. Lou gave birth to two boys, but that didn't stop her from exploring with Herbert. She put the babies in baskets and followed him wherever he went.

Their business made them a fortune, and they settled in London. Lou learned to be a gracious hostess. Herbert soon entered public service, and in 1917 they returned to the United States. Lou continued to share in Herbert's work. She used her talent for organization to help do charitable deeds.

But her concerns were also political. Ahead of her time, Lou believed in women's equality and the right of her sex to be as involved in politics as men. She didn't hesitate to express her opinions on public issues, including the need of every American for a good public education, and the right of women to have their own athletic programs. She felt so strongly that women should work that she called housewives "lazy."

Herbert's election as President didn't quiet Lou. She was more than energetic— she could shake people up. As First Lady, she was open about her sympathy for the plight of blacks. She called on women to have careers and urged boys to help with the housework. The first First Lady to make a radio address, she publicized her favorite cause, the Girl Scouts.

But for all her talk, Lou was a proper lady. She never contradicted Herbert and never tried to steal the spotlight from him. As one reporter wrote, she "was of great aid to her husband, yet remain[ed] completely in the background."

Fifty-three-year-old Lou also threw herself into that most traditional of First Lady roles—redecorating the White House. She was an active hostess, too, entertaining despite the hard times that hit after Herbert took office. With her passion for music, she invited top artists to the White House to play. Dressed often in blue or gray, and wearing no makeup or jewelry, she presided over lavish parties for which the Hoovers themselves partly paid.

Lou expected the staff at these events to do their jobs perfectly. Being First Lady had made her a fierce taskmaster. She wouldn't speak to the staff during a party or dinner, instead giving instructions by dropping a handkerchief or signaling by hand. When there were no social functions, Lou told the staff to stay out of sight. She installed a system of bells that rang when she or the President approached certain rooms. As soon as the bells went off, the staff had to leave the area.

This kind of behavior made many Americans think the Hoovers didn't care

Lou Hoover in the geology laboratory at Stanford University

about ordinary people. It was felt that Lou and Herbert just didn't understand the effects of the Depression. But the truth was that both the President and First Lady realized times were bad. They simply didn't know what to do about it. To them, relieving the country's suffering was less a matter of politics than of personal charity. They generously used their own money to build housing for the poor, even going so far as to construct a school for one community. But as President, Herbert was unwilling to involve the government and change economic policy.

Americans came to blame the hard times on the Hoovers. Still, Lou was shocked when Herbert lost his reelection bid. It turned out, though, that she loved retirement. The couple returned to California, where Lou kept hiking, biking, and camping into her sixties. Her charitable work continued, and she became president of the Girl Scouts. Herbert called her "a symbol of everything wholesome in American life."

The good times didn't last long, though. Lou died suddenly of a heart attack in 1944. Herbert outlived her by twenty years, never remarrying.

ANNA ELEANOR ROOSEVELT ROOSEVELT

wife of the thirty-second President, Franklin Delano Roosevelt

Born 1884, died 1962
First Lady 1933–1945

No one who knew the young Eleanor Roosevelt thought she was headed for greatness. Her mother thought she was ugly. Her relatives feared no man would give her a second look. After she married, her mother-in-law treated her like a weakling, running the newlyweds' household right down to arranging the furniture. Eleanor was raised as a woman of privilege who didn't need to know much about the world, and her keen intelligence took time to flower. As a young wife, she thought so little about social issues she opposed the vote for women. But as she grew older, Eleanor surprised her doubters. By the time she left the White House, she was the most influential First Lady in American history.

Eleanor was born into great wealth in New York City. Her childhood, however, was far from easy. Her mother was a great beauty and didn't hide her disappointment in her shy, plain daughter. Her father was affectionate and fun-loving but drank too much and was rarely home. By the time Eleanor was ten, her parents had both died and she was living with her cold, strict grandmother. The older woman sent Eleanor away to school in England, which the girl loved. But not much thought was given to furthering her education. College was out of the question—she was to be a society wife.

Only one person sensed Eleanor's promise—Franklin Delano Roosevelt, her brilliant, handsome fifth cousin. They'd known each other since she was two, and Franklin had always been attracted to her serious manner. Once, he told his mother, "Cousin Eleanor has a very good mind." He also knew marrying her would bring him political advantage. She was Theodore Roosevelt's favorite niece, and a President's blessing would certainly help his career.

When Eleanor was nineteen, Franklin began to court her. Her family was amazed. So was Eleanor. After all, Franklin seemed headed for political stardom; quiet Eleanor was the family wallflower. When he asked her to marry him, she said, "Why me? I am plain, I have little to bring you." He replied that if she were by his side, he "would amount to something someday."

Eleanor was thrilled by the proposal. But she knew that as Franklin's wife, she'd have to adjust to a political life. While she'd always had an interest in helping the needy—in fact, she had a job teaching poor immigrant children—Eleanor was ignorant about government. When she and Franklin married in 1905, she didn't even know the difference between a state legislature and Congress. "I hate politics!" she once wrote him.

Franklin's career seemed to bring out all of her insecurities. She was afraid to go out with his friends and associates for fear they'd look down on her. Her shyness left her reluctant to make public appearances. While Franklin held state office, and then became an official in Washington, Eleanor stayed home and raised their five surviving children (one had died as an infant).

Two events jolted her into the world. The first occurred in 1918, when she discovered Franklin was involved with another woman. They patched their marriage back together, but it was never the same. Eleanor began to realize she needed a life truly her own. Anxious for new interests, she joined women's organizations and educated herself about the issues of the day. She also threw herself into volunteer work with wounded World War I veterans and the poor.

The second event happened in 1921. Franklin fell ill with polio and became disabled. Depressed and discouraged, he prepared to leave public life. Eleanor wouldn't hear of it. She convinced him not to retire. To keep his name before the public, she agreed to make appearances on his behalf.

For the first time in her life, Eleanor focused on politics. Conquering her nerves, she made speeches, openly took positions on issues, and worked for the Democratic Party. To deliver talks more effectively, she even took speech lessons to lower her high-pitched voice.

A new Eleanor was born—a woman with confidence who wouldn't be quiet about her beliefs. By the time Franklin ran for governor of New York in 1928, his newly energetic wife was holding down a teaching job, running a furniture factory, editing a newsletter, doing volunteer work for several charities, and helping in his campaign. His election was the start of their partnership in politics, one that grew even stronger after he became President in 1933.

Forty-eight-year-old Eleanor had mixed feelings about the White House. She told a friend, "I never wanted to be a President's wife and I don't want it now." She brooded about how to balance her public and private lives. Even more, she worried that being First Lady would be all show and no substance. Her own person at last, she couldn't bear to be politically inactive.

So she went out and reinvented the role. It turned out to be the right time for an honest, outspoken First Lady. The Depression had hit America hard. There were millions living in poverty, with no hope of jobs. Because of his disability, it

Eleanor Roosevelt distributes gifts at a boys' home.

was hard for Franklin to travel and see what needed to be done himself. Eleanor became his legs, eyes, and ears.

Always on the go, she visited hospitals and prisons, Indian reservations and slums—places no First Lady had ever been before. She even went over Boulder Dam in a bucket! To draw attention to problems she felt government should address, she wrote a news column every day and monthly columns for women's magazines. She also gave lectures and speeches on the radio. Whatever money she made she gave to charity. Wherever she went, she said what she believed.

When World War II began, Eleanor went abroad to visit American troops. Traveling to hospitals, she spent time with the wounded, bringing messages home to their families. Her trips were dangerous, but she made them so often that Franklin gave her the code name of "Rover."

It was a good thing Eleanor didn't need much sleep. She was so restless that she used the stairs, since she couldn't bear to wait for an elevator. Part of what kept her going was her determination to help the less fortunate. She was dedicated to doing good in the world and showing Americans how well their government could serve them. One writer called her "her husband's conscience."

She was delighted with all the responsibility Franklin gave her. For his part, he relied on her judgment and intelligence. He wanted her to be the moral voice of his administration. It never bothered him that people knew she had a great influence on his policies. In fact, he often began statements of opinion by saying, "Eleanor and I . . ."

No First Lady had ever been so political. Eleanor's spirit and moral sense amazed most Americans. They felt she honestly cared about them, and they gave her their trust and love. Over the years, millions wrote to her in the White House. In one year alone, she received 300,000 letters!

But not everyone loved Eleanor. Many who were more conservative than she both mocked and feared her. They said a proper First Lady would stay home and take care of her family. Some commented that it was unseemly she had so much influence over her husband. There were whispers about their marriage, and about Eleanor's relationship with a close woman friend who was a reporter. But while some hated her and some laughed at her, no one could deny her power.

Despite her activism, Eleanor found time to run the White House, too. She was a gracious hostess who put total strangers at ease. Yet even at parties, when friends were trying to have a good time, she couldn't stop arguing politics. Her seriousness of purpose didn't allow her to let up.

Eleanor seemed to break all the First Lady rules. Instead of letting the staff wait on her, she did things herself. She served guests, and moved the furniture around on her own. Refusing a chauffeur, she drove her own car. Once, she even stopped and picked up a hitchhiker. Turning down Secret Service protection, she traveled on the same trains and planes as ordinary citizens.

She was interested in breaking down barriers for those who had been discriminated against. At a time when the races were still segregated, Eleanor openly supported civil rights. She started the National Youth Administration, a project that found jobs for young people of all colors. The first First Lady to hold press conferences, she allowed women reporters only. A firm believer in the equality of her sex, she urged that large numbers of women receive government appointments. Her passion for justice extended even to her parties. When she invited the ladies of Washington society to her White House teas, she also invited their maids.

When Franklin died in 1945, Eleanor said, "The story is over." But it wasn't. She could have retired and lived off her wealth, but the "First Lady of the World," as she was called, was unwilling to leave public life. Instead, she became a delegate to the United Nations, later becoming chairperson of its Commission on Human Rights. She was also appointed head of the U.S. Commission on the Status of Women. All the while, she lived unpretentiously, moving to a small New York apartment and taking the subway to work.

Eleanor never stopped fighting for the rights of the underprivileged. Historians consider her the greatest First Lady ever. That's why she's the only First Lady ever to be included in a presidential monument. There will surely never be another like her again.

ELIZABETH (BESS) VIRGINIA WALLACE TRUMAN

wife of the thirty-third President, Harry S. Truman

Born 1885, died 1982
First Lady 1945–1953

Bess Truman was the opposite of Eleanor Roosevelt. She not only avoided being politically active, but also refused to express her opinions publicly. An extremely private person, she stayed as far away from the press as she could. People joked that her two favorite words were "No comment." But while Bess wanted the public to think she was an ordinary housewife, the truth was that she wielded great power behind the scenes. In fact, she and her husband, Harry, were so close that she probably had more influence on his administration than Eleanor had on Franklin's.

Maybe that was because Harry was simply crazy about Bess. She had been the only girl for him ever since they'd met in a Missouri Sunday school when he was six and she was five. Bess was an adorable tomboy from one of the most prominent families in town. Harry S. Truman was the son of a debt-ridden farmer. He was so unsure of himself that it took five years for him to work up the courage to speak to her.

They went through school together. "She sat behind me . . . ," Harry said, "and I thought she was the most beautiful and sweetest person on earth." A top student, she was also a talented athlete. This blond, blue-eyed girl who was raised to be a lady happened to love ice-skating, fishing, and playing third base. She was also the best tennis player in town.

Many suitors came courting, but independent Bess was in no hurry to marry. She thought of Harry as just a friend. Her mother was relieved. She didn't think the boy was good enough for her daughter.

Bess's life changed suddenly when she

was eighteen. Her father fell on hard times. One day he shot himself in the bathtub. The family moved in with Bess's wealthy grandparents, but the comfortable surroundings didn't lessen the shock of the suicide. Bess remained a warm person with a great sense of humor, but she toughened, losing her natural optimism. She refused ever to speak about her father's death.

Harry, now a farmer himself, began to woo her. The first time he proposed, she turned him down. But seven years later, thirty-four-year-old Bess accepted. In 1919, they wed.

Soon after, Harry went into politics, and he was eventually elected to the U.S. Senate. His powerful new position didn't change the couple's ways. They lived simply, in a small Washington apartment with their daughter. Bess acted as Harry's secretary, also doing research and helping with his speeches. Strong-minded and intelligent, she was deeply involved in his career.

But when Franklin Roosevelt asked Harry to run with him in 1944 as Vice President, Bess objected. She knew the closer to power Harry came, the harder it would be to protect their privacy. To Bess, there was something unladylike about the spotlight. Even more, her daughter said,

The Truman family on the presidential train

she was the sort of person who liked to keep her "deepest feelings . . . from almost everyone's view." The night of the election, stubborn Bess wouldn't even stay up to hear the results.

Soon after Harry took office, Franklin died. Now Harry was President. A miserable Bess wrote of the White House, "I just dread being over there." At sixty, the shy woman was suddenly and squarely in the public eye. All she could think about was "this awful public life."

Few had been more reluctant to be First Lady. Sometimes, it seemed that what Bess wanted most in life was to go home to Missouri and play bridge with old friends. In the White House, or the "Great White Jail," as she called it, she entertained as little as she could. Determined to avoid attention, she refused to hold even one press conference. She insisted, "I am not the one who is elected. I have nothing to say to the public." Wearing old-fashioned dark suits and matching gloves and hat, she made herself seem duller than she was. People looked at short, plump Bess and saw nothing more than a traditional wife. So they nicknamed her "Mrs. America."

Yet she was far from a traditional First Lady. Every night after nine, opinionated Bess and Harry retired to his study to discuss political appointments and develop new policies. He rarely delivered a speech she hadn't approved, or made a major decision without consulting her. It was she who kept his terrible temper in check. The wife who said, "A woman's place in public is to sit beside her husband, be silent, and be sure her hat is on straight," was "a full partner," according to Harry, in all his dealings. He called Bess the "Boss," and "my chief adviser."

By the end of Harry's first term, Bess was more comfortable in the White

The first Truman family portrait taken at the White House during their occupancy

House. Her lack of pretension had made her enormously popular. Yet she didn't want Harry to run again—everyone, including her, thought he would lose. But when she realized how important the election was to him, she put aside her doubts. Accompanying him on the campaign trail, she acted as an adviser and helped write his speeches. On his famous whistle-stop tour, he'd appear at the back of the train and ask the crowd, "Do you want to meet the Boss?" Hat on head, corsage on her chest, Bess would come out, and the crowd would go wild. When Harry won the election, she was genuinely pleased.

But she wouldn't agree to a third term. The Trumans retired to Missouri, where she happily kept house and cooked for Harry. Fame and power hadn't changed down-to-earth Bess. She stuck to her ways till she died at ninety-seven, still one of the best-loved public figures in America.

MAMIE GENEVA DOUD EISENHOWER

wife of the thirty-fourth President, Dwight D. Eisenhower

Born 1896, died 1979
First Lady 1953–1961

To many Americans of the 1950s, Mamie Eisenhower was the perfect female role model. Utterly feminine and preoccupied with her appearance, she set new styles for American women. Regarded as the ideal traditional wife, she proudly made her husband her career. With her famous bangs, endless charm, and ladylike pink fashions, Mamie was the most popular woman of her time.

She started out life as a pampered child from a well-to-do Iowa family. The Douds led a carefree existence, traveling and being looked after by servants. But Mamie's mother was careful to teach her the value of money. Even as a teenager, Mamie was thrifty. Mrs. Doud didn't feel so strongly about education, though. Mamie did not attend college.

A high-spirited, talkative teenager, she was always well liked. She had many boyfriends, but until 1915, there was no one special in her life. Then she met young army officer Dwight D. Eisenhower, nicknamed "Ike." It was love at first sight. They wed a year later, when she was nineteen.

Being an army wife was hard for Mamie. Within a month of their marriage, Dwight had to leave home. "Mame," he told her, "there's one thing you must understand. My country comes first. . . . You come second." Mamie was miserable, but she knew she had no choice. Dwight, she confessed, was her "whole life."

With Dwight gone, Mamie's strength of will took over. She couldn't cook, but she was good with money. She took control of the couple's finances and managed all their moves, of which there were plenty. Since Dwight got transferred from post to post, they lived in twenty-nine different houses in twenty-nine years. Once they moved seven times in twelve months! It wasn't until after World War II that Mamie and Dwight finally owned their own home.

Much had happened to them by then. In 1921, their three-year-old son died of scarlet fever. Mamie was so upset she couldn't even cry. Dwight's grief was so intense he felt as if he were having a nervous breakdown. Soon their despair turned to anger—each blamed the other for the boy's death. For a while, it seemed the marriage might not survive. Then the birth of another son helped heal the rift.

Dwight began to rise in rank. Mamie was his biggest booster and his most helpful aide. More sophisticated than he was, she taught him how to get along with those in power to advance his career. Even more important, she gave him confidence. She said, "A man has to be encouraged. I think I told Ike every day how good I thought he was."

By the height of World War II, Dwight was in charge of all Allied forces. He was away from home for over three years. In the beginning, Mamie was so depressed that she couldn't get out of bed. Then she threw herself into volunteer work and recovered. But rumors swirled around their marriage. People gossiped about Dwight's relationship with another woman. Others hinted that Mamie drank too much.

The truth was that Dwight and Mamie were deeply attached to each other. He told her he had "never been in love with anyone but you." On their fortieth anniversary, he gave her a ruby heart on which was written "I love you better today than the day I met you."

After the war, Dwight was a hero. By 1952, he seemed a natural for the Presidency. But Mamie objected. She wanted a private life. "I don't understand politics," she said.

Still, always the good wife, she went along with his ambition. While behind the scenes she helped with his speeches, in public she avoided substance, focusing on charm. It worked. Voters flocked to see her. Wearing "I Like Mamie" buttons, crowds shouted, "We Want Mamie!" They sang campaign songs about her. One woman said, "She's going to get him elected."

She certainly helped. Dwight won, and, at fifty-six, Mamie was First Lady. She made her role exclusively social. With her outgoing personality, she proved a terrific hostess. But for Mamie, that didn't mean just throwing parties for

President and Mrs. Eisenhower leaving for the twin inaugural balls on January 21, 1953

politicians. Every day, she'd walk through the White House, shaking hands with tourists.

Like Bess Truman, Mamie made a point of staying out of politics. She didn't feel it was proper for women to get involved. She said, "Ike took care of the office, I ran the house." In the eight years he was President, she was in the Oval Office only four times.

That didn't mean she was without influence. Dwight relied on her judgments about people. White House management was hers and hers alone, and she ran the place as though she were a general. Barking orders at the staff, she held them to strict rules of behavior. A fussy housekeeper, she'd wear a white glove and run her hand over the windowsills to check if they'd been properly dusted.

Yet her guests always thought she was easygoing. No matter who came to the White House, she seemed genuinely pleased to see them. Even in the most awkward of circumstances, she was able to put people at ease. She reached out to all Americans, personally answering the approximately seven hundred letters a month she received. One year she shook seven hundred hands a day!

She did all this even though she had to watch her health. Mamie's heart was weak, and a sinus condition left her with poor balance. That's why she often worked in bed, lying there until noon. She ended up spending so much time there that the staff nicknamed her "Sleeping Beauty."

But when she rose, she knew how to make an impression. The "Mamie Look" changed American fashion. Women were in love with her short bangs, feminine clothes, and matching gloves, hats, and shoes. Still economical, she acquired an inexpensive wardrobe that got her named one of America's ten best-dressed women.

Her favorite color was pink. For the inaugural ball, she wore a gown covered with two thousand pink rhinestones, pink gloves, pink high heels, and a pink purse decorated with pink pearls. Almost immediately, "First Lady Pink" became the most popular color of the 1950s.

When Dwight left office, Mamie's wish for a private life came true. They retired to what she called her "dream house" on their Gettysburg, Pennsylvania, farm. At last she had plenty of time for her family and her favorite hobby, playing cards. She also took good care of Dwight, who had developed a heart condition.

Mamie's devotion to her husband never flagged. After he died, she said, "The light went out of my life." Though she lived ten years longer, she confided, "I miss him every day."

JACQUELINE (JACKIE) LEE BOUVIER KENNEDY ONASSIS

wife of the thirty-fifth President, John F. Kennedy

Born 1929, died 1994
First Lady 1961–1963

Jackie Kennedy brought high-society glamour and youth back into the White House. While she was a loving mother and attentive wife, she was also a sophisticated fashion plate. But she did more for her country than change women's styles. Not since Edith Roosevelt was there a First Lady so committed to the history of the White House and the culture of the nation. Considered by many the most beautiful First Lady, Jackie was a star with an intellectual mind.

Born into wealth, she grew up in New York surrounded by servants. By the age of five, she was an expert rider who'd taken home ribbons. When she wasn't with her horses, she was usually off reading and writing. Even back then, she had a curious mind.

Shy Jackie grew into a loner who valued her independence. Perhaps this was a reaction to her parents' divorce when she was eight. By the time she was in high school, Jackie was both a straight-A student and a bit of a rebel. The brown-haired teenager loved history and the arts but was also headstrong and disobedient. She became known as "the very worst girl in the school."

After college and a stay in Europe, Jackie worked in Washington as a photo-journalist. In 1951, she met a handsome congressman at a dinner party. Jackie and John F. Kennedy (who was also called Jack) liked each other well enough, but it took over a year—and the end of her engagement to another man—before they started seeing each other seriously. They married in 1953, after John's election to the Senate.

Right away the couple ran into

trouble. Jackie had no interest in politics—she hadn't even voted until John came into her life. What she valued most was privacy, not fame and power. But John's whole world was politics: he wanted to be President.

Then there was money. John was shocked by Jackie's extravagance, and they argued frequently about her spending. For her part, she was deeply hurt by the time he spent with other women. It took the birth of their daughter, Caroline, to settle the marriage down.

Despite their problems, Jackie was devoted to John. Although she disliked it, she campaigned with him. Her reason was simple: "His life is my life," she said. During the 1960 presidential race, she helped with John's speeches and made frequent campaign appearances even though she was pregnant with their son John. The voters loved her.

When her husband won the election,

Jackie Kennedy speaks with reporters while visiting Paris in June 1961.

Jackie had mixed feelings. Only thirty-one, she expected to dislike being First Lady. At the inauguration, she admitted, "I feel as though I have just become a piece of public property."

Her solution was to make the job fit her interests. In under a year, Jackie turned the White House into the cultural capital of the nation and threw herself into restoring its rooms to their original splendor.

A lover of the arts, Jackie brought the world's best musicians, writers, and artists to the White House. By making the President's home the country's cultural center, she focused the public's attention on the importance of the arts in national life. The White House became a place of refinement and intellect. Everyone wanted to be invited there.

Jackie was also intent on restoring the White House. To her, it was an important national symbol that had fallen on hard times. "It looks like it's been furnished by discount stores," she commented. So Jackie started the White House Restoration Project.

To make the building what she called a "living museum," she hunted down original furnishings belonging to past Presidents. Combing through the White House basement, she discovered furniture representing each historical period. "The White House belongs to the American people," she declared, and persuaded Congress to make it a national museum.

In 1962, Jackie brought Americans into a White House they had never seen before. She appeared live in the TV special *A Tour of the White House with Mrs. John F. Kennedy*. Over forty-eight million people watched her as she guided viewers into rooms previously closed to the public. In her high, whispery voice,

The Kennedy family on Easter Sunday, 1963

without benefit of a script, she explained their history and the artistry of their furnishings. For the first time in decades, Americans had a sense of pride in their national home.

They were also consumed with curiosity about their elegant First Lady. Reporters followed her everywhere,

though she was desperate for time on her own. Her need for privacy just increased the public's fascination.

Jackie had an impact far beyond her own country. She was a symbol of fashion and culture throughout the world. A well-educated woman who spoke three languages, she thrilled

Jackie Kennedy traveled extensively as First Lady, going as far as India.

foreign audiences when she addressed them in their own tongue. In France, she was so popular that the President introduced himself to reporters as "the man who accompanied Jacqueline Kennedy to France." When she traveled to India and Pakistan, people there called her the "Queen of America." John referred to her as his "number one ambassador of goodwill."

Whatever she did, she did without concern for politics. She herself said, "What I really want is to be . . . a good wife and mother." Later, she commented, "If you bungle raising your children, I don't think whatever else you do well matters very much." She and John adored their boy and girl, and were distraught when a third child died two days after he was born.

Her time as First Lady ended all too soon. On November 22, 1963, John was assassinated, with Jackie sitting beside him in the presidential limousine. Despite her terrible grief, she led the nation's public mourning, planning every detail of his funeral and arranging for the eternal flame at his grave.

Six years later, Jackie wed Aristotle Onassis, an older man of immense wealth. The public was disappointed—many felt she had married for money. Their union was unhappy and ended with his death in 1974.

Jackie returned to New York. Still dedicated to the arts, she worked as a book editor and actively promoted the cause of architectural preservation. When she died of cancer in 1994, she was mourned throughout the world.

CLAUDIA (LADY BIRD) TAYLOR JOHNSON

wife of the thirty-sixth President, Lyndon Johnson

Born 1912
First Lady 1963–1968

Aside from Eleanor Roosevelt, Claudia "Lady Bird" Johnson was the most politically effective First Lady of the twentieth century. Her skill stemmed in part from what she learned from her husband, a master politician. But she brought her own strengths to the job as well—a keen mind, Southern charm, and determination. No other First Lady was so dedicated to the conservation of America's natural beauty. One of Washington's first environmentalists, she used her power to put her convictions into action.

Those who knew Bird (as she was called) when she was a youngster probably found it hard to picture her in a position of political power. She was timid and insecure as a girl. To outsiders, it appeared she had everything—her father was a rich businessman in a small Texas town. But her childhood was unhappy because she was lonely. Her mother died when she was just five, and she was raised by her aunt and the family servants. Her nickname came from her nursemaid: little Claudia, the woman exclaimed, was "purty as a ladybird."

Serious, smart Bird loved books and classical music. By the time she was fifteen, she'd graduated from high school. After getting a journalism degree from the University of Texas, she worked as a reporter. Despite her wealth, she dressed plainly and lived frugally. Slow to make decisions and by nature quite cautious, she had a plan for every predicament that could arise. She didn't seem able to gather herself and do what she really wanted, which was to travel.

But that all changed dramatically when a friend introduced her to Lyndon

Johnson in 1934. A ball of fire who was secretary to a congressman, Lyndon was determined to marry her by their second date. Bird, who'd never rushed into anything, couldn't believe it. "I thought it was some kind of a joke," she said.

Nevertheless, she and Lyndon wed only two months after that date. Everything happened so quickly Lyndon forgot to bring a wedding ring to the ceremony!

Bird was swept up into Lyndon's life. He had great ambition and wanted a seat in Congress. Since she knew very little about politics, he began to teach her. He also told her what was expected of a politician's wife. Bird learned to be a gracious hostess, even though she'd never cooked a meal before. She began to dress more stylishly, wearing what Lyndon suggested: the colors red and yellow and high heels. "What pleases Lyndon pleases me," she said.

In 1937, Lyndon got his chance at Congress. It was Bird who financed his campaign, with money she borrowed from her father. Since it wasn't considered proper for women in Texas at that time, she didn't campaign with him. But she found the election thrilling. By the time Lyndon joined the navy in World War II, Bird had learned enough about the workings of Congress to run his office while he was away. She loved it.

It was right around then that she made a particularly shrewd business move, using her inheritance from her long-dead mother to buy a small Texas radio station. As Lyndon's political fortunes soared and he was elected to the Senate, Bird not only raised their two daughters but built a multimillion-dollar communications enterprise as well. Her fortune became the financial backbone of his career.

It also gave them a comfortable life.

Despite this, their marriage was difficult. Lyndon was a moody man. He'd yell at Bird in front of people, often criticizing her clothes and makeup. With little or no notice, he'd bring home large groups of people and expect Bird to quickly serve them an exquisite meal.

No matter how Lyndon behaved, Bird found the strength to put up with it. She rarely lost her temper. Even if he betrayed her with other women, Bird stood by him, uncomplaining. There were those who thought she was wishy-washy, but they didn't know her well. As one friend described her, Bird had a "touch of velvet and the stamina of steel."

Everyone seemed to like her—even Lyndon's political enemies. Her gentle manner and frequent use of colorful Southern expressions could charm even the toughest of reporters.

By 1960, Lyndon was the Democratic vice presidential candidate. Bird was determined to campaign actively for the ticket. She took speech lessons to improve her delivery in front of crowds. Traveling 35,000 miles and charming the voters, she was such an effective vote getter that Democratic politicians called her their "Secret Weapon." Some felt it was Bird who won Texas that year.

After John Kennedy's assassination, Lyndon assumed the Presidency. Fifty-year-old Bird took over the White House. Her Southern hospitality made her a successful hostess. But while she entertained frequently, her energies were focused on weightier things.

Bird was a woman who had always loved nature. She hated seeing the wilderness destroyed and the American landscape scarred. So she started the "Beautification of America" project, one of the first national environmental

President Johnson looks on as Lady Bird plants a tree.

programs. She was largely responsible for convincing Congress to pass the Highway Beautification Act, which prevented billboards and trash from ruining highways and scenic routes. Traveling across the country with her message, she planted trees everywhere to keep America green.

She did more. A strong advocate for civil rights, Bird pushed for more women to hold government positions. On behalf of her husband, she traveled through America's poorest regions to see if poverty programs were effective. "I like," she stated, "to get out and see the people behind the statistics." To carry on Jackie Kennedy's work, she sat on the Committee for the Preservation of the White House. She was also the honorary chairwoman of the educational program Head Start, and began the First Lady's Committee for a More Beautiful Nation's Capital.

Bird was always busy. There was a big sign on her office door: MRS. JOHNSON AT WORK. As First Lady, she traveled hundreds of thousands of miles, giving 164 speeches and making over seven hundred appearances. She played a vital role in Lyndon's 1964 election campaign, delivering 47 speeches in a solo whistle-stop tour of the South.

Although Bird never spoke out publicly on controversial issues, she didn't hold back in private when Lyndon asked for her opinion. He consulted her on a range of issues, saying, "I listen to her more than to any person I know." It was her advice that he followed when he decided not to run again in 1968.

Bird and Lyndon retired to Texas. After he died, she stopped appearing in public but continued to fight for the issues in which she believed. As one of her friends said, "Bird would be only half alive if she divorced herself from politics."

Her reputation has continued to grow. Historians rate her the greatest First Lady after Eleanor Roosevelt and Abigail Adams.

THELMA CATHERINE PATRICIA (PAT) RYAN NIXON

wife of the thirty-seventh President, Richard M. Nixon

Born 1912, died 1993
First Lady 1969–1974

Pat Nixon had the unfortunate distinction of being the only First Lady whose husband resigned from office. But then, she had learned about heartbreak and suffering early in life.

Pat's family was so poor she was born in a tent. Her father just eked out a living on his California farm, and the little girl spent much of her time doing chores to help him. When she was thirteen, her mother died, and things got even worse. It fell to Pat to care for the house and her two brothers. She remembered later that when she was "a youngster, life was sort of sad."

But Pat was smart. Despite all her responsibilities, she was a good student. Then just as she graduated from high school, her father died. The teenager was crushed. "I don't like to think back to that time," she once remarked.

Pat had no money, but she was determined to go to college. "I always wanted to do something else besides be buried in a small town," she said. She worked her way through the University of Southern California as a sales clerk, a dental technician, a telephone operator, and a movie extra. Even with her hectic schedule and money worries, she graduated with honors and landed a job teaching typing in high school.

She met Richard M. Nixon, a young attorney, at tryouts for a town play. He instantly fell for her and her radiant smile. Although they hadn't even gone out on a date yet, he told her, "Someday I'm going to marry you." She confessed later, "I thought he was nuts." But Richard knew what he wanted: he courted Pat for two and a half years. When they married in 1940, it looked as if she'd finally left the bad times behind.

A few years later, Richard ran for Congress. Pat didn't care for politics but went along with his decision. She said, "I could see it was the life he wanted." To finance his campaign, she sold part of her father's farm and also gave him the money she'd been saving to buy them a home.

It turned out the election appealed to Pat's ambition. She became involved in the campaign and helped write Richard's literature. Although public appearances made her nervous, she campaigned by his side. They'd drive to rallies in their station wagon, and Richard would pull down the back, climb onto it, and address the crowd. Pat would walk among the people and give away thimbles. She avoided politics whenever she spoke, commenting only on what she did around the house. The voters loved it. The Nixons became known as the "Pat and Dick" team.

Richard was elected to the House, and then to the Senate. Pat worked in his office and continued to campaign with him. Yet her doubts about his career didn't fade. While she enjoyed all the traveling a political couple did, she felt she should be at home raising their two daughters. When she pressed Richard to give up politics, he wouldn't.

The longer his career lasted, the more uncomfortable Pat became with it. But she was a loyal wife who stuck by her husband. In 1952, he was elected Vice President. Suddenly, she was squarely in

President and Mrs. Nixon on the White House lawn

the spotlight. Forced to mix frequently with large groups of people, she was so ill at ease she came off as stiff and cold. While Pat was charming and fun-loving in private, in public she seemed unemotional. Some people called her "Pat the Robot" and "Plastic Pat." Most Americans, however, appreciated her sincerity and hard work.

In 1960, the political pressure on her grew worse. Richard ran for President on the Republican ticket. To take advantage of Pat's popularity, the party staged a "Pat Nixon for First Lady" week. Richard bragged, "We've always been a team."

In a close and bitter campaign, Richard was defeated. Pat was disappointed but took comfort in his departure from politics. She was looking forward to a quiet life.

Yet, just two years later, he ran for governor of California. Pat was so upset at first that she refused to help him. As a friend said, "She hated the idea of ever facing another campaign. Every time Nixon entered one she was in deep despair." But once again, Pat stuck by him. She said, "A man has a right to make his own decision about his career and a woman should support that decision." When he was defeated, she wept.

As the years passed, the endless political strain seemed to take a toll on Pat. She became thin and drawn and grew even more anxious. She and Richard began to argue. He didn't consult her on important decisions. In 1968, days passed before he even told her he was running for President again.

In a replay of the past, Pat objected but Richard paid no heed. Yet she shared his joy when he won, even though, at fifty-six, she had to be First Lady.

There were times Pat enjoyed the job. She visited eighty-three countries,

becoming the most widely traveled First Lady ever. Following in Jackie Kennedy's footsteps, she busied herself with redecoration and doubled the number of historic pieces of White House furniture. Her ideal was to make the building truly available to the public, so she started the Christmas candlelight tour, the garden tour, and tours for the blind.

Pat enjoyed being a hostess, especially when women's organizations visited the White House. Believing strongly in the power of the individual to make a difference, she tried to convince Richard to nominate a woman to the Supreme Court. But she had little influence on him. One reporter said, "Mrs. Nixon had these ideas, but [the President] wouldn't let her do anything about them." It didn't help that Richard's staff disliked her and drove an even deeper wedge between them.

The sadness that shadowed Pat's life returned during Richard's second term. He was at the center of the greatest presidential scandal in history: Watergate. He tried to cover up crimes by associates, and then lied about it. Pat protested his innocence and tried to stay calm. But the stress and humiliation of the accusations made her withdraw into herself.

Richard was forced to resign, and he and Pat retreated to California. For a while, Pat was so depressed she didn't go out. She became known as the "lonely lady of San Clemente," the town in which they lived. Still, many Americans admired her for standing by her husband.

In 1976, Pat had a stroke and never appeared in public again. Her distrust of politics had proven true. She died in 1993.

ELIZABETH (BETTY) BLOOMER WARREN FORD

wife of the thirty-eighth President, Gerald Ford

Born 1918
First Lady 1974–1977

Betty Ford once said, "Being ladylike does not require silence." That just may have been her motto. Far from being a distant figure who served her husband's career, Betty spoke openly about her personal problems, even revealing to the public that she had breast cancer. Suddenly Americans, particularly women, realized they could discuss their troubles without shame. Although Gerald Ford was President for only two and a half years, Betty changed how people thought about the First Lady. She was no longer a mere public figure but a human being.

Betty was a woman who had always done things her own way. Growing up in Michigan, she was "a terrible tomboy," as she described herself, trying to play football and hockey like her brothers. By eight, though, she'd become so fascinated by dance she called it "my happiness." At fourteen, she was teaching it to children in a neighbor's basement. To earn extra money, the attractive teenager also modeled for a department store.

In love with the arts and determined to dance with the best, twenty-year-old Betty moved to New York and joined the Martha Graham Company, a prominent modern dance group. She soon found, however, that the hard work and concentration required of a professional dancer caused her to sacrifice everything else in her life. When her mom pressured her to come home, Betty agreed.

She returned to Michigan and again taught dance. She also became the fashion coordinator for a department store. When she was twenty-four, she wed a salesman named William C. Warren.

The marriage was a failure. By the time she was twenty-nine, she was divorced and unsure if she'd ever marry again.

Just before her divorce was final, Betty met Gerald Ford, a lawyer. The two of them agreed to date casually. But six months later, in 1948, he proposed and she accepted. During their engagement, they didn't see very much of each other: "Jerry," as he was called, was running for Congress and was totally absorbed in the race. In fact, he was so involved in his campaign that he was late to their wedding!

Gerald won the election, and became an important figure in the Republican Party. As the years passed, the marriage took a backseat to his career. Though she did her best to become a good political wife, by the time he took over as House Minority Leader, Betty said, "I was feeling terribly neglected." While Gerald was away an average of 258 days a year, Betty took care of their home and four children. Even though they talked on the phone every day, she couldn't help feeling Gerald was more attached to his work than to her.

She was very unhappy. Then an injury to her neck made her feel even worse. That's when she decided to fight back. She went to see a psychiatrist and regained her sense of self-worth. Then, to help save her marriage, she convinced Gerald to retire from politics.

She hadn't counted on Watergate, however. When Nixon's Vice President, Spiro Agnew, had to resign because of corruption charges, Congress approved Gerald to take his place. Even Betty was excited—she knew this was a great opportunity for them both. Just eight

The Ford family in the White House

months later, President Nixon resigned, too. Gerald was Chief Executive. When he was inaugurated, he said, "I am indebted to no man and only to one woman—my dear wife."

At fifty-six, Betty became the first First Lady whose husband had never been elected as either President or Vice President. She didn't care. She was thrilled to be in the White House. Right away, she livened it up. Dressed to the nines, she loved to throw parties and entertain artists and royalty.

Being First Lady brought out the best in Betty. She was one presidential wife who wasn't afraid to openly disagree with her husband. A warm but blunt woman who said what she thought, she was more liberal than Gerald and often found herself in trouble with his party. "I do not believe being First Lady should prevent me from expressing my ideas," she stated, and her husband agreed.

Those ideas were controversial: Betty was a feminist. She believed in the right of women to have abortions, and supported the Equal Rights Amendment (a proposed amendment to the Constitution preventing discrimination against women). When it was defeated, she focused on helping women get appointments to higher office. She was so active in pursuing her causes she needed a staff of twenty-eight people to help out.

But perhaps her greatest contribution to American life came in the form of her frankness. She was forthright about her own emotional distress and helped educate people about an illness that was rarely discussed back then: breast cancer. Only a few weeks after Gerald became President, Betty discovered she had a lump in her right breast. The breast had to be removed. Rather than keep the news secret, Betty made it public. Because of her, millions of women became aware of the disease and began to go to their doctors for checkups. By choosing not to keep a personal crisis private, Betty ended up saving thousands of lives.

No matter what Betty said, Gerald supported his wife. He often consulted her, even though his advisers feared her views would cost him votes. They were wrong. Even those who differed with her respected her for speaking her mind. They agreed when she said, "I felt the people had a right to know where I stood."

By the time Gerald ran for President in 1976, Betty was more popular than he was. At his rallies, people wore buttons reading "Elect Betty's Husband" and "Keep Betty in the White House." He said, "If I could just get my rating up to hers!"

But he couldn't. Betty was distraught when Gerald was defeated. She knew she'd badly miss being First Lady. After the Fords left the White House, Betty grew depressed. Her arthritis (a swelling around the joints) worsened, and she began taking pills to kill the pain. She also began to drink heavily. Her worried family helped her get treatment for prescription drug and alcohol abuse.

True to form, Betty confessed her problems to the public. It's not for nothing that she's stated she wants to be remembered "for being able to communicate with people." But she didn't just talk—she took action. She helped found the Betty Ford Center for Drug and Alcohol Rehabilitation, one of the best addiction-treatment centers in the world.

When she first became First Lady, Betty said, "They can't make me be somebody I'm not."

She was right, and her country is grateful for it.

ELEANOR ROSALYNN SMITH CARTER

wife of the thirty-ninth President, Jimmy Carter

Born 1927
First Lady 1977–1981

Rosalynn Carter never had a doubt about being First Lady. After leaving the White House, she exclaimed, "I enjoyed every minute of it." Sometimes known as a "steel magnolia," since she combined Southern charm with toughness, she was nearly as workaholic as Eleanor Roosevelt and had even more influence on her husband. An equal partner in both her marriage and her husband's political career, Rosalynn reported that she and Jimmy "always worked together on everything." They were so close it seemed to strangers they could read each other's thoughts. Jimmy knew he was a lucky man, and never hid how much he depended on her.

But then, Rosalynn was always the kind of person people could rely on. Growing up in the small town of Plains, Georgia, she was the oldest in a family that had to work hard to make ends meet. A responsible child, she was always doing chores. She was such a good little girl that she would wear a white dress all day and not get a speck of dirt on it.

When Rosalynn was thirteen, her adored father died. For a long time after, every day was a struggle. "We were poor," Rosalynn remembered. To support the family, her mother took in sewing and worked at the post office. By fifteen, Rosalynn had a job in a beauty parlor to help out. She was growing up quickly— her mother treated her like an adult and always asked for her advice.

But Mrs. Smith also made sure her daughter got an education. She saved money to send Rosalynn to junior college. She knew her daughter was smart, so smart that she was her high school class valedictorian. By the time

Rosalynn was in her freshman year at college, she'd begun to dream of the day she'd leave the South behind.

In the summer of 1945, after her first year at Georgia Southwestern College, Rosalynn started dating her best friend's brother, Jimmy. While she had known him all her life, just as everyone in a small town knows everyone else, he was older than she and had been away at school for four years. He was pursuing a career as a naval officer and was about to enter his last year at the Naval Academy when he fell in love with Rosalynn. They had a lot in common. Both were bright, religious, and from the same town.

The two wrote to each other every day. Yet the first time Jimmy proposed marriage, Rosalynn turned him down. "I wasn't ready to get married so soon," she said. But he persisted, and she had a change of heart. They wed in July 1946 when Rosalynn was nearly nineteen.

Navy life meant the couple had to move from base to base. To make matters worse, Rosalynn was often alone while Jimmy was at sea. But over the years, she adjusted. She found she loved being a navy wife—it gave her a chance to see the world. "I would wake up all excited about the day ahead," she remarked.

Everything changed, however, when Jimmy's father died. Jimmy decided to leave the navy and go home to run the family peanut-farming business. Rosalynn objected. She couldn't stand the idea of being stuck in a small town again. "I did everything to make him change his mind, but I couldn't do it," she said. Back in Georgia, she was depressed for months.

Then Jimmy asked her to help run the business. Rosalynn quickly came back to life. Her husband needed her, and she rose to the challenge. So while she raised their four children, she also took care of the finances for their farm supply business.

When Jimmy went into state politics, she was delighted. Soon he was governor, and Rosalynn began learning how to help people in need through government. She developed a special interest in assisting mentally ill youngsters. Just as she'd always been, she was her husband's adviser. There was only one way in which she failed to help him: she couldn't address large audiences. Public speaking made her physically ill.

That changed when Jimmy ran for President. He was a complete unknown at the time, and the Carters realized they had to get his name before as many voters as possible. So they campaigned separately. Rosalynn traveled to nearly a hundred cities on her own, returning home only on the weekends. She found the experience thrilling. It boosted her self-confidence, and she became comfortable delivering speeches.

With Rosalynn's help, Jimmy was elected President. After the inauguration, they walked hand in hand down Pennsylvania Avenue to the White House. It was a signal to Americans that this was one President who had a partner in power. Rosalynn believed the First Lady should help improve the country, and she was determined not to let her opportunity go to waste. Making clear from the start she would be more than a gracious hostess, she stated, "I would not like supervising the entertaining and hospitality, and the domestic running of the White House, to become my main priority."

She was forty-nine years old, and she knew what she wanted. "I was determined to be taken seriously," she said. She tried to get Congress to do more to help

The Carters volunteer to help build homes for the poor in Chicago.

the mentally ill and the elderly. Like Betty Ford before her, she urged passage of the Equal Rights Amendment. She supported legislation to improve Social Security and was the honorary chairperson of the President's Commission on Mental Health, testifying before Congress on national mental health policy.

But Rosalynn's interests and influence extended beyond that. She worked closely with her husband on foreign policy and diplomatic matters. They scheduled regular working lunches and discussed policy whenever they were together. She was such an important part of Jimmy's administration that she attended cabinet meetings and met with heads of state on her own. Perhaps his most trusted adviser, she often edited his speeches and helped plan political strategy. Rosalynn, Jimmy felt, understood the needs of average Americans better than he did.

They were true soulmates. He once called her "almost a perfect extension" of himself. No wonder, then, that her influence on him was so great. But while there were some Americans who felt uncomfortable with her power, Rosalynn never had ambition for herself. All her energy and activism were directed at helping her husband and her country.

Decades after Jimmy's 1980 defeat, she's still working to help people in need around the world through The Carter Center, in Atlanta, Georgia, a non-governmental organization the Carters founded to wage peace, fight disease, and build hope. There, Rosalynn continues to devote her time to improving the lives of those with mental illnesses as well as to projects to wipe out terrible tropical diseases and to encourage democracy through free and fair elections. Americans admire this former First Lady whose life is an example of service to others. As was true in the past, Rosalynn is someone people can count on.

ANNE FRANCES (NANCY) ROBBINS DAVIS REAGAN

wife of the fortieth President, Ronald Reagan

Born 1921
First Lady 1981–1989

Nancy Reagan brought extravagance back to the White House. Not since Jackie Kennedy was a First Lady so fashion-conscious and stylishly dressed. Unlike Rosalynn Carter, Nancy believed her job was to be the ultimate hostess, so she lavishly redecorated and threw expensive formal parties. Nancy's dream was to make Washington glamorous again.

She did, but it meant spending millions at a time when Americans throughout the country were suffering economically. The contrast with the moneyed White House was too much for many people. Nancy was often criticized—even mocked—although she raised private funds to pay some of her expenses. One magazine went so far as to label her the "idle rich . . . obsessed with fashion and society." She became a symbol of everything critics felt was

wrong with the administration.

Yet Nancy was only living the way she always had. From the first, she was raised in well-to-do circumstances. She went to top schools and was surrounded by the best of everything.

But her family's money couldn't buy Nancy happiness or security. Her parents divorced when she was just two, and she barely saw her father again. Her mother pursued an acting career and left little Nancy with relatives for five years. It was not until she was seven that she began to have a true family life. That was when her mother remarried and retired from acting.

Nancy adored her stepfather, a prominent neurosurgeon. They were so close that she would go to the hospital and watch him operate on patients. She seemed to pick up her political values from him: he was a conservative Republican, just as she turned out to be. She loved him so dearly that when she was fourteen she asked him to adopt her. When he did, she took his name.

Pretty young Nancy also followed in her mother's footsteps. In high school, she was the president of the drama club and then majored in drama at Smith College. Just a few months after graduation, she landed a role in a Broadway show. Soon she was on her way to Hollywood.

Nancy ended up making eleven movies. She was a successful actress leading a glamorous life. Yet she wasn't completely happy. Her "even greater ambition," she confessed, was to get married.

In 1949, she met the actor Ronald Reagan at a dinner party. It wasn't love at first sight—they dated for two and a half years. But Nancy waited patiently, and in 1952, they married. She felt that her real life was beginning at last.

Very quickly, she ended her career. Nancy had "no desire," she said, "to continue as an actress once I became a wife. . . ." She was determined to be a devoted spouse and mother. It was fortunate that she had the money to hire good help—not only was she unable to cook a meal, but she once admitted that she couldn't even boil water!

Over the next six years, the Reagans had a son and a daughter. Nancy also helped raise her husband's two children from his previous marriage. But it was always "Ronnie," as she called him, who was the true center of her life. When he ran for governor of California, she was by his side every time he delivered a speech. Nancy didn't accompany him just for show: she was a keen judge of character and helped out in the campaign.

When Ronald was elected, Nancy discovered that there was little privacy in political life. Reporters demanded interviews, and those who disliked her felt free to criticize her. So she was less than enthusiastic when he decided to run for President.

Yet she plunged into the campaign with tremendous energy. At every opportunity, she boosted Ronald's confidence, advising him about strategy and experts he might hire. He relied on her so heavily that one of his associates stated that she was as "responsible for [his] success as he."

No one was prouder than Nancy when Ronald won the election. She busied herself planning the most lavish inaugural celebration ever (it became known as the "Big Bucks Inaugural"). Yet when she thought about being First Lady, the fifty-nine-year-old Nancy confessed to a friend, "I'm so scared." The job seemed overwhelming.

Nancy had never been active politically on her own. Her major goal had always been to protect Ronald from the stresses of his career (the 1981 attempt on his life made her even more committed to doing so). Trying to avoid controversy, she made up her mind to do what she knew best and plunged into redecorating the White House family quarters. She bought a new set of china for over $200,000. "I believe very strongly," she said, "that the White House is a special place and should have the best of everything."

But economic times were hard. Americans were shocked at her expensive tastes. The press began to refer to her as the President's "number one public relations problem." Others poked fun at her, calling her "Queen Nancy." They laughed when it was reported that she spent two months planning one state dinner.

Nancy felt the criticism was unfair. But she knew that unless she changed her image, she might damage Ronald politically. So she began to use her great sense of humor to make fun of herself in public. She set to work studying past First Ladies to see how they handled the job. Developing an interest in drug prevention, she started the "Just Say No" campaign. She still entertained, but she'd expanded her role, saying, "I don't know how you could be in this position and not grow. You're in the middle of history."

As the years passed, the country realized that Nancy was far more than a hostess. As one of Ronald's most influential advisers, she could change his mind about an issue or see to it that someone she disliked was fired. She said, "Although I don't get involved in policy, it's silly to suggest that my opinion shouldn't carry some weight with a man I've been married to for thirty-five years." She was so much a part of the way he made decisions that when he was operated on for cancer in 1985, she announced she was "the President's stand-in."

Nancy and Ronald were so close that they hated to be separated. The Reagans made more joint appearances than almost any other presidential couple. To express his gratitude for all she'd done for him, the President declared in one speech, "Nancy is my everything."

Then the glamour and the power ended. The couple returned to California and to private life. But it was not a happy retirement: Ronald developed Alzheimer's disease (an illness in which nerve cells deteriorate and the brain shrinks, destroying the mind). Through his decline, Nancy was by his side. Now Americans will best remember her for her true devotion to her fading husband.

Ronald and Nancy Reagan on Ronald's eighty-ninth birthday

BARBARA PIERCE BUSH

wife of the forty-first President, George Bush

Born 1925
First Lady 1989–1993

White-haired Barbara Bush seemed like everybody's grandmother. At sixty-three, she was one of the oldest First Ladies ever, with a warm manner that disguised an often sharp tongue. She was so comfortable with herself she felt no need to project the glamour and high style of Nancy Reagan. Instead, she expected the public to take her as she was, informing her husband's campaign advisers, ". . . I won't dye my hair, change my wardrobe, or lose weight." Americans sensed her honesty and loved her down-to-earth manner. From the beginning of their White House stay, "Bar," as she was called, was more popular than George.

She would rather have had it the other way around. Barbara never had much personal ambition. She was devoted to George Bush and his work. Ever since they'd met at a Christmas dance when she was sixteen, her life had been focused on him. He was the first boy she'd ever kissed.

In those days, Barbara lived in New York, the tall, brown-haired daughter of a successful businessman. She was an average student, with no interest in a career. What she wanted was a husband, and she and George were engaged by the time she graduated from high school. When he returned from fighting in World War II, she dropped out of Smith College to become his wife. It was 1945, and Barbara was all of nineteen years old.

Life with George proved to be hectic. The couple moved from Connecticut to Texas so George could try his hand at the oil business. After achieving great financial success, he became involved in politics and was elected to Congress in 1966. Still, the Bushes didn't settle down. Over the years, his political ambition led to various government and Republican

The Bush family

Party appointments. He was often away, leaving Barbara with their six children to raise and frequent relocations to manage. But she was so well organized the moves went smoothly. In all, the family lived in twenty-nine different houses in seventeen different cities before the White House became their home.

The marriage was a happy one, although it was touched early by tragedy. Their daughter Robin was stricken with leukemia and died when she was nearly four. It was then that Barbara's hair began to turn white.

The couple's immense grief brought them closer together. George often confided in Barbara about his work. Although she considered herself a housewife and was frightened of public speaking, she freely discussed political strategy with her husband and had great influence over his decisions. She hated the years he headed the CIA (Central Intelligence Agency). Because his work was top-secret, he couldn't consult with her.

Barbara's life changed dramatically once her children were grown. Suddenly, she had time to consider her own interests. Affected by feminism's call for self-fulfillment, she volunteered to assist in programs to improve Americans' literacy (the ability to read). She had a strong personal commitment to the issue, since one of her sons had had a disability that made learning to read hard. When George became Vice President, Barbara turned the fight for literacy into her special cause.

That remained true after George's election to the Presidency, when Barbara drew the nation's attention to the fact that millions of Americans couldn't read. So passionate was she about the problem that, as First Lady, she established the Barbara Bush Foundation for Family Literacy.

She embraced other causes as well. The "Silver Fox," as her children called her, spoke out on the problem of homelessness, and hugged AIDS patients to show the disease wasn't contagious. While she took care to avoid speaking publicly on most controversial issues, privately Barbara was "blunt and opinionated," one reporter claimed. Disagreeing with both the Republican Party *and* her husband, she was known to support the Equal Rights Amendment, and to be sensitive to the concerns of minorities, women, and gays. She was especially interested in the rights of Hispanics, since one of her daughters-in-law was Mexican.

As always, Barbara had tremendous influence on George. Though it wasn't obvious to the public, he constantly relied on her advice. The two got up at six and ate breakfast together, reading the newspapers and watching the news on TV. Barbara cut out articles for him to read, helped with his speeches, and sat in on political strategy sessions. One reporter wrote that Barbara "weigh[ed] in on everything from policy to personnel." An aide to the President said the couple "shared everything."

But it was her personality, not her intelligence, that made Barbara so popular. Not the least bit embarrassed about her age or her appearance, she called herself "everybody's mother" and made jokes about how old she was. She was so unpretentious she even knitted at congressional hearings. A naturally informal person, she'd walk her dog along Pennsylvania Avenue in her robe and slippers.

Determined not to be trapped by her official role, Barbara often went out on her own with friends, visiting museums and shopping at malls. Every day she went swimming and played tennis. Americans appreciated her relaxed manner and sense of humor. Barbara was such a hit with the voters she received up to three thousand letters a week.

When George was defeated for reelection, Barbara was bitter about the loss. Still, she was glad to get out of the public eye. Now she's enjoying her fourteen grandchildren, her garden, and the new President, whose election made her the first First Lady since Abigail Adams to see both a husband and a son become President.

Barbara Bush reads to children at the National Learning Center.

HILLARY DIANE RODHAM CLINTON

wife of the forty-second President, William Jefferson (Bill) Clinton

Born 1947
First Lady 1993–2001

No First Lady has been more controversial than Hillary Rodham Clinton. Her husband's political opponents criticized her almost as often as they did him, accusing her of everything from financial corruption to running the White House to being a political radical. Yet no matter what history concludes about her years as First Lady, Hillary earned a unique place for herself in the annals of her country: she was the first First Lady to have an established career of her own and the first to run for public office. In 2000, Hillary ran for the U.S. Senate in New York. She set out her own political positions, not her husband's, and took to the campaign trail herself. No First Lady had ever been more ambitious or eager to serve in her own right.

From childhood on, Hillary had been taught to be independent and successful.

Her mother raised her as the equal of her two brothers and hoped aloud that she would sit on the Supreme Court one day.

Her father, temperamental and tough, constantly pushed her to be the best. The owner of a drapery business, he was a right-wing Republican, so tightfisted that he wouldn't heat the house at night. He held blond, blue-eyed Hillary to such a high standard that he was rarely pleased with anything she did. Once when Hillary brought home a report card full of A's, he told her, "That must be an easy school you go to."

This lack of praise seemed to spur Hillary on. She was a top student and skilled athlete, with a take-charge personality. Always proper, she'd sometimes wear her Girl Scout uniform to class. In Park Ridge, the Chicago, Illinois, suburb in which she lived, she was known as a leader who believed in conservative politics and wanted to do good. By the time she graduated from high school, Hillary was deemed "most likely to succeed."

Yet her energy and drive masked a natural shyness and insecurity. She was so embarrassed by her thick eyeglasses she'd often refuse to wear them. When she didn't recognize classmates because of her poor eyesight, they thought she was an icy snob. Perhaps that's why her high school newspaper once predicted she'd end up a nun named "Sister Frigidaire."

At Wellesley College, Hillary continued to be at the top of her class. She was a young woman who paid less attention to her social life and personal appearance than to politics and the ideal of public service. One professor called her the most outstanding student he'd ever taught.

It was in college that Hillary truly became her own person. She left her father's conservatism behind and embraced liberal politics. The shift began when she tutored poor African-American children, observing lives of real hardship for the first time. The Vietnam War, the assassinations of Robert Kennedy and Martin Luther King, Jr., and the civil rights movement deeply affected her. When she graduated from Wellesley in 1969, she challenged Republican values in her rousing graduation speech. It got her her first national publicity, a story in *Life* magazine.

Committed to serving those in need, Hillary went on to Yale Law School. There she became involved with the Children's Defense Fund and decided to specialize in the rights of children. She helped to establish one of the nation's first child-abuse reporting systems.

In her second year at Yale, Hillary overheard a young man chatting in the student lounge. They noticed each other immediately but didn't speak. Weeks later, in the law library, she realized the same young man was watching her. Marching up to him, she declared, "Look, if you're going to keep staring at me and

One hundred days after President Clinton was sworn in to office,
Hillary Rodham Clinton dominates the newsstands.

Hillary Rodham Clinton officially announces her plans to run for Senate.

I'm going to keep staring back, I think we should at least know each other's names. I'm Hillary Rodham." He was Bill Clinton.

The two had much in common: a love of politics, faith in government, and ambition. Excited by her brilliance, Bill also brought out her sense of fun. In just a few months, they were in love and living together.

After law school, Hillary became an attorney for the Children's Defense Fund, then worked on the investigation of the Watergate scandal. Bill returned to Arkansas. To be with him, in 1974 Hillary took a job teaching criminal law at the University of Arkansas School of Law. She started the school's first legal-aid clinic, providing free representation for the poor.

When Bill ran for Congress, Hillary became his closest political adviser. She believed in him so deeply that she told friends he would be President one day. The admiration was mutual. Bill called Hillary "the smartest person I ever met in my lifetime."

He lost the election but got the girl. In 1975, he and Hillary married. In 1978, he was elected governor and Hillary became Arkansas's First Lady. She didn't give up her career, even after daughter Chelsea's birth in 1980. The first woman lawyer and later the first woman partner at Arkansas's most prestigious law firm, Hillary was so successful that she was twice named one of the top hundred lawyers in America by *American Lawyer* magazine.

Chelsea's birth was a difficult one.

Hillary was warned by her doctors not to have another child. More bad news followed. Bill's popularity had sunk, in part because of Hillary. Arkansans picked her apart for not wearing makeup, dressing in unfashionable clothing, and keeping her own last name. They were shocked that she earned more money than her husband. They disliked her liberal views even more.

Bill lost the next election, in 1980, and Hillary went into action. She changed her wardrobe, her haircut, and her name. Out went the eyeglasses, in came the contact lenses and makeup.

It seemed to work. Bill was reelected in 1982. He appointed Hillary to head a committee to reform Arkansas schools, then the nation's worst. The changes she proposed became the basis for a national model and helped propel Bill into the spotlight.

She was a major force in his 1992 presidential campaign, continuing to act as one of his key political advisers and standing by him when he was accused of having an affair. Bill was open about Hillary's influence. He stated, "Vote for one, get one free." When Americans elected Bill, they seemed to approve of the idea that a President's wife could be a partner in governing.

Forty-six when she came to the White House, Hillary was the first First Lady to be a genuine policymaker. Combining her duties as wife, mother, and hostess with the job of heading the Task Force on National Health Care Reform, she proposed legislation to change the health care system and make insurance available to millions without it. She did not merely influence policy behind the scenes; she openly made it.

But her program was defeated. Her popularity dived. Political opponents accused her of being power-hungry and too liberal for the country's good. Some voters grew uncomfortable with her independence; to them it made her seem unfeminine. Others found her arrogant and cold. They knew about her temper, but not her warmth or sense of humor.

Republicans went on the attack. Hillary was accused of financial and political wrongdoing on several fronts. But after years of investigation, no charges could be brought.

Hillary was never cowed by the controversy swirling around her. While she changed her hairstyle often and softened her manner to seem more feminine, she never hid her power or her importance. She used her position as First Lady to draw attention to a wide variety of causes: women's right to abortion, greater funding for breast cancer research, a Patients' Bill of Rights, equal pay for women, gun control, and children's rights. She wrote a best-selling book, *It Takes a Village*, about her beliefs, and started Save America's Treasures to preserve important historical sites.

In 1998, Hillary stood by the President when he was impeached, in part for lying about his relationship with a woman named Monica Lewinsky. Hillary was used to the rumors about Bill and other women. Despite his behavior, she always accepted his apologies and forgave him. Voters sympathized with her pain and admired her strength.

When she left the White House, Hillary didn't forget the lesson her parents had taught her: to be tough in the pursuit of excellence. Like her hero Eleanor Roosevelt, she longed to excel in public service, and as the first First Lady elected to public office, the new Senator from New York has achieved her dream.

LAURA WELCH BUSH

wife of the forty-third President, George W. Bush

Born 1946
First Lady 2001–

From the start of her time in the White House, it was easy to see that Laura Bush had two things in common with another First Lady—her mother-in-law, Barbara Bush. Both women loved the new President, George W. Bush, the first son since John Quincy Adams to follow his father to the Oval Office. And both shared a passion for helping Americans learn to read. Like Barbara before her, Laura was dedicated to the campaign for literacy.

She had always been interested in education and reading. A quiet, shy only child, Laura discovered books early in life and loved to read. She was also drawn to teaching and would line up her dolls to give them lessons. By the time she was in second grade, she had made up her mind to become a teacher. It made sense: well-organized, disciplined, and neat, Laura

was an excellent student who felt at home in school.

She was a Texas girl who grew up in the oil town of Midland. Her family lived comfortably—her father owned a real-estate business. The Bush family lived nearby, and she and George went to the same grade school. Back then, though, the two barely knew each other.

In high school, blue-eyed Laura seemed more mature than most Midland girls. While in some ways she was a typical teenager, hanging out with friends at the local drugstore and listening to rock and roll, she was unusually focused for her age. Always an attentive student, Laura was as determined as ever to be a teacher. Her glasses even helped her look the part!

But a horrible event marred those years. When she was seventeen, Laura

Laura Bush reads to kindergarten students in Flowood, Mississippi.

accidentally drove her car through a stop sign, smashing into a passing vehicle. The driver—a friend of hers—was killed in the crash. Laura recalls this as "a very tragic time in my life."

The accident didn't sway her from her goal, however. Entering Southern Methodist University, Laura majored in education. After graduation, she achieved her childhood dream, teaching grade-school classes in Dallas, Austin, and Houston. Her favorite part of the job was reading to her students, and she soon realized that she'd like to become a librarian, too. So she went back to school, and in 1973 she was awarded her master's degree in library science from the University of Texas at Austin.

Laura was happy and successful in her career. In 1977, friends tried to fix the thirty-year-old up with an attractive, out-going oilman—George W. Bush. For a while, Laura refused. The little she knew of George made her think they had nothing in common. After all, he was a politically ambitious Republican, and as Laura said, she was "uninterested in politics." When forced to take a position, she called herself a Democrat.

But her friends believed she and George would make a perfect couple. They planned a barbecue to introduce the two in June, and Laura finally agreed to go.

Her friends were right. That night, George talked and talked, and Laura, always a good listener, ended up having a great time. She was charmed by his energy, and he was taken with her calm, confident style. A whirlwind courtship followed, and by the day after her birthday in November, they were married. George now says it "was the best decision I ever made."

There was no time for a honeymoon, however. George was running for Congress, and Laura immediately joined him on the campaign trail. She hated it. A private person, she felt uncomfortable in the public eye. Realizing that, George vowed she'd never have to give a speech on her own. But just a few weeks later, in 1978, he had to break that promise.

A rally had been scheduled that George couldn't attend. He begged Laura to go in his place. She nervously agreed, quickly memorizing some lines. She had no trouble at the start, stating, "My husband told me I'd never have to make a political speech. So much for political promises." Then her mind went blank. After a minute and a half of fumbling for words, she just sat down. It took her years to become a relaxed campaigner.

Not that that bothered Laura. After George lost the election and she settled into being a homemaker, she had more important things on her mind. Although the Bushes desperately wanted children, Laura had a hard time getting pregnant. When she finally did, the pregnancy left her so ill she had to be hospitalized. But she felt that the birth of her twin daughters, Barbara and Jenna, in 1981, made the risk to her health worthwhile.

In the mid-1980s, the Bush marriage went through a rocky time. It was a period when George was unsuccessful in business and politics, and his unhappiness led him to drink excessively. Laura strongly disapproved. She urged him to

quit, but he didn't seem able to. Finally, she gave him a choice. As George later revealed, "Laura said, 'It's me or the bottle.'" In part to save his marriage, he gave up alcohol in 1986.

No one who knew Laura was surprised she got tough with George. She was quiet, but as one friend said, she could "hold his feet to the fire." With her no-nonsense nature and strength of character, she helped him mature.

Laura wasn't enthusiastic when George decided to run for governor of Texas in 1994. Happy with her life with "Bushie," as she called him, she worried that in the statehouse, she wouldn't have time to do the things she loved best— raise the twins, garden, and read. She was also reluctant to give up her family's privacy. But George was determined, and Laura agreed to help. She was delighted for him when he earned his first political victory.

Unpretentious Laura found herself First Lady of Texas. Although, as one friend said, she had "steadfastly refused to pursue the limelight," Laura realized her new position gave her the chance to follow her dream once again. From the statehouse, she could help people learn to read.

So, dressed in stylish tailored suits, she began to give speech after speech on the importance of literacy. "Reading is to the mind what food is to the body," she declared. During George's governorship, Laura became one of the state's most effective First Ladies ever, organizing the Family Initiative for Texas, a campaign to improve community literacy programs, and starting the Texas Book Festival, a celebration of literary achievement in the state, which raises funds for public libraries. She also helped promote the arts and raise awareness of women's

President-elect Bush and future First Lady Laura Bush enter the chambers of the Texas House of Representatives in Austin, Texas, on December 13, 2000.

health problems, particularly breast cancer.

Despite George's success as governor, Laura didn't want him to run for President. She knew that once they were in the White House, it would be even more difficult to keep their lives private. George would be subject to criticism, and she wasn't sure how she'd react. Her daughters, whom she'd always protected, would inevitably be written about in the press. She herself wasn't sure how she felt about a new role. "I've always done what really traditional women do, and I've been very, very satisfied," she stated.

But George was eager to run. Laura felt she owed it to him and her country to agree. Throwing herself into the 2000 election, the once-awkward speaker proved to be an effective campaigner.

Now, after the closest election of modern times, the fifty-four-year-old is First Lady. She's determined to use her skills to push anew for literacy. "Education is dear to both of our hearts," Laura says of herself and her husband as she pursues her lifelong vision of teaching people to read.